Cambridge Elements ≡

Elements in the Philosophy of Law
edited by
George Pavlakos
University of Glasgow
Gerald J. Postema
University of North Carolina at Chapel Hill
Kenneth M. Ehrenberg
University of Surrey

REVISITING THE RULE OF LAW

Kristen Rundle
University of Melbourne

CAMBRIDGE
UNIVERSITY PRESS

Shaftesbury Road, Cambridge CB2 8EA, United Kingdom

One Liberty Plaza, 20th Floor, New York, NY 10006, USA

477 Williamstown Road, Port Melbourne, VIC 3207, Australia

314–321, 3rd Floor, Plot 3, Splendor Forum, Jasola District Centre,
New Delhi – 110025, India

103 Penang Road, #05–06/07, Visioncrest Commercial, Singapore 238467

Cambridge University Press is part of Cambridge University Press & Assessment,
a department of the University of Cambridge.

We share the University's mission to contribute to society through the pursuit of
education, learning and research at the highest international levels of excellence.

www.cambridge.org
Information on this title: www.cambridge.org/9781009009676

DOI: 10.1017/9781009000512

First published 2022

A catalogue record for this publication is available from the British Library.

ISBN 978-1-009-00967-6 Paperback
ISSN 2631-5815 (online)
ISSN 2631-5807 (print)

Cambridge University Press & Assessment has no responsibility for the persistence
or accuracy of URLs for external or third-party internet websites referred to in this
publication and does not guarantee that any content on such websites is, or will
remain, accurate or appropriate.

Revisiting the Rule of Law

Elements in the Philosophy of Law

DOI: 10.1017/9781009000512
First published online: December 2022

Kristen Rundle
University of Melbourne

Author for correspondence: Kristen Rundle, kristen.rundle@unimelb.edu.au

Abstract: This Element offers an accessible introduction to theoretical writing on the rule of law. Part 1, 'Approaching the Rule of Law', examines the methods through which the idea of the rule of law is typically approached by those who set out to theorise it. Part 2, 'Untangling the Rule of Law', asks whether it is possible to untangle the rule of law from the various contributions, companions, connections, conflations, and controversies with which it tends to be associated. Part 3, 'Revisiting the Rule of Law', signals to new frontiers of rule of law thought by addressing the assumptions about legal form that shape its theoretical treatment, and by investigating what is known about the people who carry its burdens and benefit from its offerings.

This Element also has a video abstract: www.cambridge.org/rundle

Keywords: the rule of law, legal theory, political theory, mutual subordination to law, officials and subjects

ISBNs: 9781009009676 (PB), 9781009000512 (OC)
ISSNs: 2631-5815 (online), 2631-5807 (print)

Contents

Introduction

To dare to invoke the phrase 'the rule of law' is to expect to be asked what exactly one means to convey by doing so. Offering a basic answer such as that the rule of law refers to a condition in which government and citizens alike are subject to the law is likely only to satisfy for a moment. There is simply more to the idea than that.

Theoretical endeavour associated with the rule of law has been around for centuries. Why, then, has engagement with the idea become more complex in recent years? One answer is that the last four decades have seen an exponential increase in scholarly engagement with the rule of law in response to a range of 'real world' developments within which the idea has been assigned a central place. The political and legal transitions precipitated by the collapse of communism in Eastern Europe are considered by many to be the primary catalyst, alongside the effort of international organisations such as the International Monetary Fund to make rule of law compliance a condition of engagement with countries dependent on their financial assistance. Analyses of worldwide trends of 'democratic decay' have also highlighted apparent abuses of the rule of law as an indicator of that malaise. The rule of law has, it seems, been doing a lot of work because it has been given a lot of work to do.

In an ideal world, visitors to this crowded landscape would be given a roadmap to help them find their way in. That roadmap would explain that any given engagement with the rule of law will be shaped by particular starting points, particular aims, particular methods, and have particular obstacles with which to wrestle, as well as particular conclusions to offer. It would also emphasise that any such engagement is just one of many possibilities for the same. Sadly, it is much more common for those encountering scholarly engagement with the rule of law to have to figure these things out for themselves, nervous about the holes in their understanding, and wondering what tools could have helped them to have a better run of it.

About This Element

The aim of this Element is to provide some of those tools. As a contribution to the Cambridge Elements series on the 'Philosophy of Law', its goal is to offer an accessible introduction to theoretical writing on the rule of law.

This Element's brief provides a refreshing opportunity to make this offering by leading with questions and themes rather than with the works of particular scholars. The three-part design of the Element is accordingly intended to foreclose the possibility that the experience of encountering the rule of law will be set by any one theorist's mode of presenting the idea, or their motivations for doing so. Its aim instead is to promote awareness of the historical, political, institutional, and cultural contexts within which all theoretical writings on the rule of law are situated, and which explain much about why particular treatments of the idea take the shape and carry the content that they do.

Part 1, 'Approaching the Rule of Law', examines the methods through which the idea of the rule of law is typically approached by those who set out to theorise it. All approaches to the rule of law implicate foundational choices about how this task is best pursued. Becoming aware of the methodological patterns that cut across different kinds of scholarly engagement with the rule of law is therefore important not only for its own sake, but also for anticipating the vocabularies and sites of focus likely to be found – or neglected – within different 'theories of' the rule of law.

Part 2, 'Untangling the Rule of Law', moves beyond the idea of the rule of law, standing alone, to examine the entanglements within which it is often situated. The primary objective of this part is to ask whether it is possible to untangle the rule of law from the various contributions, companions, connections, conflations, and controversies that have come to be associated with it, and to consider what might follow for our understanding of the idea from an attempt to do so.

Part 3, 'Revisiting the Rule of Law', takes up the Element's invitation to signal to new frontiers of rule of law thought by asking what might still be missing or under-examined within theoretical engagement with the idea, and why. Though a number of inquiries at the boundaries of orthodox rule of law thought could have comprised the focus of this exercise, attention is directed to two underdeveloped areas in particular: the assumptions about legal form that shape theoretical treatment of the rule of law, and what we know (and don't know) about its people – the often disembodied figures through and upon whom the work of the rule of law is thought to be done.

Designed in this way, the overriding objective of this Element is to engage readers in an exercise of noticing and seeing that builds on itself, piece by piece, over the course of the three parts. One consequence of organising the Element this way is that certain questions or themes that might ordinarily travel together within single works are examined at different locations across the three parts. When the works of individual scholars are brought into focus, the purpose of doing so is to emphasise contributions from or features of those works that address or otherwise illuminate the issues under examination. Intersecting connections are highlighted where relevant, and references cited should be taken as representative only.

The timing of the writing of this Element was serendipitous, insofar as it coincided with the arrival of a number of other stocktaking or perspective-seeking works on the rule of law. To avoid repeating the efforts of others, readers are directed to those other works when it is helpful to do so. Though not explicitly intended as a companion to a companion, this Element might fruitfully be read in conjunction with the *Cambridge Companion on the Rule of Law* (Meierhenrich & Loughlin, 2021), a much larger volume that offers valuable insight into the breadth and depth of theoretically inflected scholarship on the idea of the rule of law at this point in its history.

Finally, a word about audience. The rule of law is a working idea that is given meaning and application in everyday discourse and practice. Responsibility for shaping what is carried by the idea has never been the preserve of scholars alone, and never will be. It is for this reason that although aimed principally at students and teachers of legal and political thought, this Element has ultimately been written for anyone who wants to understand more about how we think, speak, and write about the rule of law, wherever it might appear.

1 Approaching the Rule of Law

1.1 Five Vignettes

Every approach to the rule of law must start somewhere. For students of the idea, that starting point is typically one or other vignette drawn from the work of a particular scholar. Sometimes that vignette will read as if offering an answer to the question 'what is the rule of law?'. At other times it might be expressed as a description of what the rule of law aims to do, or of what it requires or is meant to prevent. Consider the following five examples:

> For all the power the government has, being only for the good of society, as it ought not to be *arbitrary* and at pleasure, so it ought to be exercised by *established and promulgated laws*: that both the people may know their duty, and be safe and secure within the limits of the law, and the rulers too kept within their due bounds. (Locke, 1982: 85, emphasis in original)

> No man is punishable or can be lawfully made to suffer in body or goods except for a distinct breach of law established in the ordinary legal manner before the ordinary Courts of the land. In this sense the rule of law is contrasted with every system of government based on the exercise of persons in authority of wide, arbitrary, or discretionary powers of constraint. (Dicey, 1897: 179–80)

> Stripped of all technicalities, this means that government in all of its forms is bound by rules fixed and announced before-hand – rules which make it possible to foresee with fair certainty how the authority will use its coercive powers in given circumstances and to plan one's individual affairs on the basis of this knowledge. (Hayek, 2007: 112)

> The rule of law consists of principles that constrain the way government actions change and apply the law – to make sure, amongst other things, that they maintain stability and predictability, and thus enable individuals to find their way and to live well. (Raz, 2019: 2)

> The Rule of Law is one of the ideals of our political morality and it refers to the ascendancy of law as such and of the institutions of the legal system in a system of governance. (Waldron, 2016)

These five vignettes are a just sample of the kinds of theoretical statements that could provide the starting point of an approach to the rule of law. Together they span several hundred years of reflection about the idea, and some striking commonalities cut across them. To begin, each conveys a message about power being possessed and exercised in a particular way, namely: through law. 'Arbitrariness' is a consistent worry, and stability and predictability are lauded. People knowing what 'rulers', 'government', or 'the state' expects of them is another recurrent theme, while several make specific demands such as that the laws that rule come in the form of 'rules', 'announced beforehand', 'publicly made', and so forth. But there are differences, too. Notice how the first three vignettes are framed negatively, oriented to the ills that the rule of law is thought to prevent, while the last two are less clear on this front (indeed the fourth might be thought to have a distinctly positive flavour). Only some speak to who or what is bound by the rule of law, or to who stands to benefit from it.[1]

We unpack, elaborate, and complicate these observations over the course of this Element. The point for immediate purposes is that each of the five vignettes is *theoretical* because each seeks to sharpen our understanding of the rule of law at the level of the idea itself. Yet on their own, presented as little more than a sound bite, vignettes of this kind tell us little about what it means to produce a theory of or otherwise to engage theoretically with the idea.

Our concern in this first part of the Element is with this question of method. Our objective is to better understand *how* theories of and theoretical engagements with the rule of law are pursued, packaged, and expressed. But before we embark on this examination, we need to address the fact that scholarly engagement with the rule of law often takes for granted that the reader comes armed with an awareness of the recurrent ideas and vocabularies through which its investigation is typically handled. Much risks being lost in this assumption. We begin therefore with some of the recurrent themes of the history of rule of law thought, to which we will return repeatedly throughout the Element.

1.2 Recurrent Themes

1.2.1 Political or Legal – or Both?

Perhaps the most important thing to understand about the idea of the rule of law is that it straddles political and legal thought.[2] The idea has always had these two dimensions, and it always will.

In its political dimension, the rule of law is concerned with a particular way of arranging political power, namely: that such power should be framed by, exercised through, and answerable to law. The basic idea is that both sides of the political relationship – the rulers and the ruled, the government and the governed – must each be subordinate to the demands of the law. Throughout this Element we will refer to this basic idea as the political demand of mutual subordination to law. The legal dimension of the rule of law follows readily from its political dimension in its concern for *how* the demand of mutual subordination to law is met. The focus here is on how the institutions and practices of a legal system constitute, express, and sustain that political demand.

---

[1] We return to this question in Section 3.3.1.

[2] That there is a boundary between legal and political thought – at least at the level of theory – is itself a contested question among philosophers: Murphy (2014: 61–88).

Our primary concern in this Element accordingly lies with how the rule of law is thought to frame political rather than interpersonal relationships, that is, relationships between ruler and ruled, or government and governed, rather than those between and among persons generally.[3] The political–legal mix represented in the idea of the rule of law can produce some interesting differences between how it is approached by scholars of political and legal thought, respectively. Those who approach the idea from the starting point of legal thought often take its political demands as given and concentrate instead on the granular details of how those demands might manifest in actual legal arrangements. Conversely, those who approach the rule of law from the starting point of political thought often play down the significance of those granular details to the fate of its claimed connections to liberty (Section 2.2.2) or other core concerns of political theory. Neither approach is necessarily wrong. Both are however necessarily incomplete. The best counsel for those approaching the rule of law, therefore, is always to keep in mind that the idea has both political and legal dimensions, and that one or other of those dimensions (more often than both) might be pushed to the foreground within any particular engagement with it.

1.2.2 'Arbitrary' Power

Fear of tyrants and of tyranny has always been central to claims about the functions or purposes of the rule of law. This explains much about why, for centuries, we have been invited to understand the idea by reference to its apparent opposition to the rule of man, or men.[4] More often, however, the historical core of rule of law thought has been associated with a much more specific 'anti-hero' (Krygier, 2019: 761): the possibility of arbitrary power or rule.

'Arbitrary power' is an idea in its own right, and scholars of the rule of law have devoted considerable effort to reflecting on its possible meanings.[5] At its simplest, the idea speaks to patterns in the exercise of power that cannot be anticipated by those who are subject to it. The worry here is primarily about unpredictability, from the point of view of the person subject to power so

---

[3] Put differently, our primary focus is on the vertical as opposed to horizontal dimensions of the rule of law. The mutual subordination idea could however be redirected to capture the idea that the rule of law subordinates all relations in a polity, public and private, to a framework of law.

[4] This formulation of the problem is often attributed to Aristotle (2016: 89): 'it is thought to be just that among equals everyone be ruled as well as rule, and therefore that all should have their turn ... And the rule of law, it is argued, is preferable to that of any individual.'

[5] Theorising arbitrary power is especially important to teleological theorists of the rule of law: see Section 1.4, and especially Krygier (2019), and Krygier (2017: 150) where it is suggested that there are at least three kinds of arbitrary power relevant to the rule of law – power that is uncontrolled, power that is unpredictable, and power that is un-respectful. Compare the approach of those working within the philosophical framework concerned with reasons for action, and for whom arbitrary power is 'the use of power that is indifferent to the proper reasons for which power should be used': Raz (2019: 5); see also Raz (1979: 219–20).

exercised. But being also about power, the term 'arbitrary power' equally communicates something important about to subjection to the whims of another, in the mode of untrammelled domination.

The question for our preliminary purposes is what an emphasis on arbitrary power within a particular theoretical engagement with the rule of law might indicate about how the latter is being perceived. Here we might especially notice the typical connection between a concern for arbitrary power and 'negative' conceptions of the rule of law. That is, if the purpose of the rule of law is understood to be prevention of or protection from arbitrary rule, it is easy to see the link between this understanding and the dominant orthodoxy of rule of law thought that associates the idea with freedom *from* the encroachments of political power.

This does not mean, however, that understandings of the rule of law that locate arbitrary power at their centre are incompatible with more positive framings of the idea. One recent engagement that maintains an emphasis on arbitrary power, for example, argues for an association between the rule of law and a way of acting 'with a manifest intention to protect and advance the interests of the governed' (Raz, 2019: 13). The point is simply that the directions of thought opened up by the traditional emphasis of rule of law theory on arbitrary power are not necessarily settled. At the same time, that emphasis is very likely to shape – in often significant ways – the next level of claims about what the rule of law is or requires.[6]

1.2.3 'Rule of Law' versus 'Rule by Law'

One of the distinctions to which scholarship on the rule of law returns repeatedly is the asserted difference between rule *by* law and the rule *of* law. Both ideas refer to political orders in which law is given a central role in the project of government. So, what is the idea of the rule of law doing that rule by law is not?

We might begin to unpack the claimed difference between these two types of law-based political rule by reflecting on the message conveyed by their 'of' and 'by', respectively. The key point here concerns the direction of legal obligations. Rule by law says nothing about the legal obligations of the ruler, beyond the need to comply with the formal strictures necessary to govern through law. This is why the term is generally associated with a type of political rule in which law is a tool with which government can do as it pleases (Tamanaha, 2004: 96; Waldron, 2016: 4), and why it is often used in connection with what are sometimes described as 'authoritarian' political regimes (Ginsburg & Moustafa, 2008; Rajah, 2014: 4; Seppänen, 2016). The message conveyed by the rule of law, by contrast, is that the obligations of law

---

[6] See further Section 3.4.2.

apply equally to *both* ruler and ruled. Both are mutually subordinate to the demands of law.

The rule of law/rule by law distinction is not merely an evaluative device for assessing whether a given political order is best described in terms of one or the other. The distinction – roughly – also describes the historical difference between the kind of political rule that emerged through English traditions of government, and that associated with the European tradition of the *Rechtsstaat* (law state). In this historically situated version of the distinction, law in the rule of law tradition acts primarily as a constraint on political power, while law in the *Rechtsstaat* (rule by law) tradition acts primarily as its conduit or means of rule (Meierhenrich, 2021: 57). The shorthand '*Lex, Rex*' neatly captures this difference.[7] In the rule of law tradition, '*Lex*' (law) is prior to '*Rex*' (the sovereign) because the sovereign must govern through *and* be answerable to law. In the *Rechtsstaat* tradition, by contrast, '*Rex*' (the sovereign) comes before '*Lex*' (law) because law is the sovereign's instrument of rule.

Yet like all distinctions, this one is bound, if not to break down then at least to lead a complex life. In practice, most political orders will reside somewhere on a spectrum between the rule of law and rule by law, generally or in relation to specific instances of governance. But there is also a philosophical objection to the distinction. Even if in a political order best described as one of rule by law those in power want to use law as nothing more than a tool through which to wield that power, it is not just any kind of tool. It is law, and it can only be law if it complies with the demands that make law a distinctive tool of governance. Thus, this objection asks: are these demands not themselves a distinctly legal constraint (even) on those who seek to use law as no more than a tool of power? The point is that even if these demands of legality might not be so strong as to make *all* instances of legal governance instances of the rule of law rather than rule by law, the better approach might be to position the two along a continuum of legal constraints on political power, rather than as polar opposites (Dyzenhaus, 2022).

1.2.4 Idea or Ideal?

It is common across contemporary theoretical approaches to the rule of law to see it described as an 'ideal'. Sometimes this point is taken further, with the rule of law positioned as only one ideal among others that a given political order might strive to meet: democracy, respect for human rights, and economic freedom are often cited as examples (Raz, 1979: 210–11; Waldron, 2016: 1).

---

[7] This illuminating formulation was devised by Friedrich Hayek, the author of our third vignette (see the helpful explanation in Meierhenrich (2021: 47–56). We return to Hayek's rule of law in Section 1.5.2.

What we need to grasp for preliminary purposes is what describing the rule of law as an 'ideal' tells us about the *kind* of idea it is thought to be.[8]

An ideal is a *normative* idea: a projection about how things should be, rather than about how they are as a matter of fact. Designating the rule of law as an 'ideal' is a way of saying that it is not a thing, like a chair, or a dog. Rather, it is an aspiration, or a goal – something we must work to (try to) achieve. It is widely accepted that, despite its importance, the rule of law rarely will be fully realised in practice. Just how far practice can depart from the demands of the rule of law and still lay claim to being an instance of it, however, is a significant point of dispute among theorists of the idea. The point for immediate purposes is simply that whether the rule of law can be said to be present will always require evaluation, by whatever measures are designated as relevant to that evaluation.

There are also other implications for theorising the rule of law that arise from its status as an ideal. Starting from the assumption that the rule of law is an aspiration, for example, might encourage us to abstract it from time and place. It is precisely this kind of theoretical idealism that has seen some scholars call for greater historical sensitivity within theories of the rule of law, explicitly (re) locating the idea within the specific political and legal conditions that inform different theories about it (Shklar, 1987).

1.2.5 An 'Essentially Contested Concept'

It is in the nature of normative ideas that their meaning is contested and contestable. It is hard to think how it could be otherwise: aspirations are worth aspiring to for different reasons to different people. There accordingly will never be complete agreement on what the rule of law is, what exactly it demands, or why it matters. This is why it is commonly described as an 'essentially contested concept'.

There can be confusion about what exactly this label means. An essentially contested concept is something much richer and more complex than an idea whose meaning is hard to agree upon. In its proper philosophical usage, an essentially contested concept is a theoretical designation that draws attention to 'the way in which arguments about the meaning of a given concept contribute to our understanding and evaluation of the systems, practices, and actions to which the concept is applied' (Waldron, 2021: 121). In relation to the rule of law specifically, therefore, the designation of essentially contested concept is a way of showing 'how the heritage of disputation associated with it enriches and

---

[8] See Marmor (2010) for a longer analysis of the methodological puzzles that come with the designation of the rule of law as an ideal.

promotes some or all of the purposes for which the rule of law is cited in legal and political argument' (Waldron, 2021: 122).[9]

The key point about the rule of law as an essentially contested concept, then, is that to approach it is to *expect* disagreement about its meaning, content, benefits, burdens, and much besides. Although this inevitably means that working with the idea can be challenging, the designation 'essentially contested concept' is not meant to discourage us from doing so on the basis that we will never entirely win the argument. Quite the opposite, properly understood, that designation invites us to walk towards the idea of the rule of law with openness towards its possible content and application in a given circumstance, fully aware that others may have different views, but undeterred by any of those things. Indeed, some have suggested that the inherent lack of agreement about the content of normative ideas like the rule of law can be a source of their strength, insofar as their contestability might unite people in supporting the idea in principle even if they cannot agree on precisely what it is meant to designate (Raz, 2019: 3).

1.2.6 'Theories Of' or 'Theoretical Engagements With'?

Writings on the rule of law are often grouped together as if there is no difference between those we might label theories of the rule of law and those that might better be described as theoretical engagements *with* the idea. To some extent this may be right. In this Element, however, where relevant, one description is used rather than the other to point out how scholars have different ways of and different reasons for working with the idea. However imperfect the distinction might be, labelling a particular theoretical treatment of the rule of law one way or the other is a way of drawing attention to what is going on within an encounter with it.

Our focus in the remainder of this first part is primarily on theories of the rule of law: writings that purposefully set out to offer an account, definition, or statement of the rule of law as an object of inquiry in its own right. Elsewhere in the Element, and especially in our examination of the entanglements within which the idea is often situated, the themes and works examined might better be described as theoretical engagements with, rather than theories of, the rule of law.[10]

The key takeaways of this brief survey of recurrent themes of rule of law thought might be summarised as follows. The rule of law is an idea whose meaning is and will always be contested, which is often understood as much in terms of what it is not as what it is, and which, being aspirational in character, might never be fully realised in practice. Its historical lineage is associated with

---

[9] See Waldron (2021: 129–34) for an explanation of the philosophical puzzles associated with the designation 'essentially contested concept' and its genesis in the work of W. B. Gallie.

[10] See Sections 2.1 to 2.6.

the particular role assigned to law in English rather than European traditions of political rule, and as a subject of theoretical treatment it is sometimes the object of inquiry and at other times merely part of it. Our task now is to become acquainted with how the rule of law tends to be approached when positioned as the object of inquiry in its own right.

1.3 'Accounts' of the Rule of Law

The most common assumption about what it means to produce a theory of the rule of law is that the objective is to provide an account of the idea. The label 'account' tends to be used quite loosely in rule of law talk, as if any enterprise of theorising the idea is an account-giving endeavour. Properly understood, however, account-giving is a particular method for theorising an object of inquiry that is associated with the enterprise of analytic philosophy. Within this methodology, an account is usually presented as a list of the features that the object of inquiry *necessarily* must have, or of the criteria that it necessarily must fulfil, to be an instance of the thing or practice being examined. Account-giving so understood usually also attaches to the idea that the object being theorised is a 'concept'. For those engaged in this enterprise in relation to the rule of law, then, the aim is to provide an account of the concept of the rule of law, untangled from its association(s) with any other concept(s).[11]

1.3.1 An Account of What, Exactly?

But what is the character of the listed features said to be necessary in a given account of the rule of law? The elements that comprise accounts of the rule of law may go by a number of different names, including 'desiderata', 'demands', or 'requirements'. The most common description of such listed features is, however, that they are an account of the 'principles' of the rule of law.

The first thing to notice in the work of those engaged in this activity is that such scholars will usually offer no more than a tentative answer to what the phrase 'the rule of law' means. Energies are instead directed to articulating the content of its necessary principles. What those principles are thought to *do*, however, is generally clear. To borrow from the fourth vignette reproduced at the beginning of this part, together the principles of the rule of law are thought to 'constrain the way government actions change and apply the law'. But what *kinds* of principles are these necessary principles of the rule of law?

This is where three familiar descriptions of rule of law theory – 'formal', 'procedural', and 'substantive' – enter the picture (Tamanaha, 2004: 91–113; Craig, 1997; Waldron, 2016: 5). Because one of the most contested aspects of rule of law theory is what place is to be accorded to each of these three categories in an

---

[11] See further Section 2.2.1.

account of its principles, it is important to understand the claimed differences between them.

The *formal* principles said to be necessary for the rule of law relate to the form that law, in a rule of law order, should take. Demands of generality, clarity, and publicity, among others, are formal principles in this sense because they speak to the required form of legal norms within a condition that lays claim to the rule of law. These formal principles tend to comprise a common foundation across different accounts, and rarely provoke controversy. It is what *else* an account of the rule of law should include that generates contestation.

The *procedural* principles thought by some to be required for the rule of law concern the processes and institutions through which legal norms are administered. Examples of such processes include requirements of natural justice or fair hearing, and the principle of innocence until proven guilty. Examples of institutions include the expectation that there will be courts, presided over by independent and impartial judges.[12]

The point of departure between formal and procedural principles, on the one hand, and *substantive* principles, on the other, is that the latter concern the content ('substance') of law in a system that lays claim to the rule of law. Only some theorists insist that substantive principles should be among those that comprise an account of the rule of law, in addition to formal or procedural principles. A classic substantive demand in contemporary rule of law theories is that the rule of law must include a commitment to the protection of human rights: a demand on the content of the law, not on its form or the procedures for its administration.

1.3.2 Examining Some Accounts

The common (if somewhat disparaging) description of accounts of the principles of rule of law as 'laundry lists' suggests that one might tick off each principle to determine whether a condition of the rule of law exists or does not exist. The purpose of reproducing three of the most well known here is not to pass judgement on their merits, but simply to notice their style, shape, and recurrent and divergent preoccupations.

Account #1

Laws should be:

1. Comprised of general rules
2. Publicly promulgated

---

[12] See further Section 2.5.1 for engagement specifically with the philosopher Jeremy Waldron's contribution to theorising the procedural dimensions of the rule of law.

3. Non-retroactive
4. Sufficiently clear
5. Non-contradictory
6. Possible to comply with
7. Relatively constant through time
8. There should be congruence between official action and the declared law.

Account #2

1. All laws should be prospective, open, and clear.
2. Laws should be relatively stable.
3. The making of particular laws (particular legal orders) should be guided by open, stable, clear, and general rules.
4. The independence of the judiciary must be guaranteed.
5. The principles of natural justice must be observed.
6. The courts should have review powers over the implementation of the other principles.
7. The courts should be easily accessible.
8. The discretion of the crime-preventing agencies should not be allowed to pervert the law.

Account #3

1. The law should be accessible and predictable
2. Legal questions should be determined according to law, not by the exercise of discretion
3. The law should apply equally to all, except where objective differences justify differentiation
4. Ministers and public officers at all levels must exercise the powers conferred on them in good faith, fairly, for the purpose for which the powers were conferred, without exceeding the limits of such powers and not unreasonably
5. The law must afford adequate protection of fundamental human rights
6. Means must be provided for resolving without prohibitive cost or inordinate delay, bona fide civil disputes which the parties themselves are unable to resolve
7. Adjudicative procedures provided by the state should be fair
8. The state must comply with its obligations in international law as in national law

These three accounts span a period of fifty years in the development of twentieth-century rule of law theory, and they can readily be seen to build on each other.[13] Account #1 is thought to contain exclusively 'formal' principles, although its eighth principle of congruence between official action and declared rule might be regarded as concerned more with prescriptions around the application and enforcement of law than with the form of legal norms (Waldron, 2008: 7).[14] Account #2 explicitly declares itself to be concerned with formal principles concerning 'the system and method of government in matters directly relevant to the rule of law' (Raz, 1979: 218). Account #3 consciously adds 'substantive' requirements to a formal and procedural base, including demands that the law adheres to human rights and complies with international law, as well as considerations affecting the character of and access to dispute resolution mechanisms.

We might also notice that Accounts #2 and #3 pay attention to the kinds of institutions expected not just to be present, but to operate well, in a political order of the rule of law kind. This development is worth dwelling on for how it indicates that different principles of the rule of law will tend to attach to particular institutions considered suited to their advancement or protection.[15] To this end, the centrality of courts to both accounts is therefore noteworthy.[16] We might also notice that all three accounts at least appear to be presented as general theoretical offerings, in the sense that they are not apparently tied to a particular place and time. That said, Accounts #2 and #3 are obviously contemporary, and vindicate the observation that even if they are presented in general terms, theories of the rule of law tend to take their complexion from the perceived problems and perceived institutional capacities of their era (Palombella, 2010: 4; Lacey, 2021: 462).

Laundry lists of the principles of the rule of law are, however, invariably just one part of their author's theoretical engagement with the idea, and are rarely intended to be read in isolation from accompanying careful explanations of and justifications for the inclusion of each feature or principle (Fuller, 1969: 46–91; Raz, 1979: 214–19; Bingham, 2010). It will invariably also be the case that such accounts will play a particular role in the larger aims of the analysis or set of arguments within which they are found. For example, the author of Account #2 emphasised the need to interpret its principles in light of what is claimed to be

---

[13] Account #1 is associated with the thought of Lon Fuller (1969: 39) – specifically his arguments about the eight principles of the 'internal morality of law' – and is dated to 1964. We return to Fuller's contribution to rule of law theory in Section 3.4. Account #2 is the work of Joseph Raz (1979: 217–18), and acknowledges its convergence with Fuller's list in some foundational respects: see further Raz (2019) for a revised and much longer list of principles. Account #3 is drawn from the work of the British jurist Tom Bingham (2010: 37–132).

[14] We revisit the idea of form within rule of law thought in Section 3.1.

[15] Institutional dimensions of rule of law theory may in turn benefit from empirical research to be fleshed out: see Taekema (2021) for a provocation to a philosophers of the rule of law to pay greater attention to empirical and doctrinal resources.

[16] We return to the significance of courts within rule of law thought in Section 2.4.

the basic idea underscoring the rule of law, namely, 'that the law should be capable of providing effective guidance' (Raz, 1979: 218).[17]

It is however important to emphasise that the work of assembling accounts of the principles of the rule of law is not done solely by philosophers. These days some of the most hardworking accounts of the rule of law are those devised by international and non-governmental organisations such as the United Nations,[18] the International Monetary Fund,[19] and the World Justice Project[20] in association with international rule of law 'promotion' and 'measurement' projects (Ginsburg & Versteeg, 2021; cf. Humphreys, 2021 and Chalmers & Pahuja, 2021). For present purposes, however, the key takeaway is this. The provision of an account of its essential features appears to have become the dominant understanding of what it means to produce a theory of the rule of law. Ultimately, however, this is just one method through which to pursue that enterprise, and is in any event likely to be only part of its author's analysis of the idea.

1.4 Teleological Approaches

For some theorists of the rule of law, the provision of an account of the so-called concept of the rule of law is the very last objective of their work. Indeed, one theoretical approach to the rule of law that has become especially prevalent in recent years – the teleological approach – positions its refusal of the account-giving enterprise at the centre of its offering. Though scholars committed to this approach share with analytical approaches the need to posit what the rule of law is, they insist that those working within that dominant enterprise ask the wrong question from there. For teleologists, asking what the rule of law is *aiming for* – its teleology, purpose, or function – must come before any anatomical inquiry into its so-called essential features (Krygier, 2008: 44–69, 2011: 64–104; Cheesman & Janse, 2019: 264–9).

The primary objection of such theorists to rule of law theoretical orthodoxy is not to the account-giving exercise per se, but to the claimed generality of accounts so produced. Teleological theorists insist that the best way to extrapolate the necessary conditions for the rule of law is to make such inquiry sociologically specific to

---

[17] See further Section 3.3.3.

[18] The United Nations (in United Nations Secretary-General, 2004: 4) famously defines the rule of law as 'a principle of governance in which all persons, institutions and entities, public and private, including the State itself are accountable to laws that are publicly promulgated, equally enforced and independently adjudicated, and which are consistent with international human rights norms and standards.'

[19] The International Monetary Fund (1996) called for '[p]romoting good governance in all its aspects, including by ensuring the rule of law, improving the efficiency and accountability of the public sector, and tackling corruption, as essential elements of a framework within which economies can prosper.'

[20] The World Justice Project's (2021) 'working definition' of the rule of law is underpinned by what it sees as four universal principles: accountability, just law, open government, and accessible and impartial justice.

particular times, places, and circumstances. If an anatomical exercise of the account-giving kind is to be pursued at all, the aim at most should be to provide open-ended working models of the rule of law, tailored to the specificities of local circumstances (Hertogh, 2016; Krygier, 2017: 133–68).

The shift in inquiry that defines the teleological approach to the rule of law – where one asks what the rule of law is aiming for, before one asks how it might best be achieved – immediately invites the question of how that aim is to be described. This explains why teleological theorists have engaged with the content and connotations of the idea of arbitrary power more extensively than other methods for theorising the rule of law (Section 1.2.2). Strictly speaking, however, an approach that prioritises the question of the purpose of the rule of law could attach to any number of different answers about the character of that purpose. Economic development, promoting human rights or any number of other responses could plausibly join 'preventing arbitrary power' as answers to the purpose of the rule of law.[21] So far, however, the preponderance of scholarship associated with the teleological approach has been preoccupied with power and measures to prevent its arbitrary exercise, or in Martin Krygier's phrase, with 'tempering power' (Krygier, 2016b: 35, 46–8; King, 2019: 365–7).

1.5 Theories within Theories

It is true for all theories of the rule of law that their surrounding context will reveal much about why they are being offered and why they take the shape and have the content that they do. For some theories of the rule of law, however, including some of the most well known, producing a theory of the rule of law was not necessarily the primary aim of their author's enterprise. This suggests that we can only properly understand some theories of the rule of law if we *also* have some grasp of the larger projects within which they are located. Two leading examples serve to illustrate this.[22]

1.5.1 A Rule of Law Theory for (English) Constitutionalism

Those who come to the idea of the rule of law through the study of constitutional law are likely to be familiar with the second vignette reproduced at the

---

[21] Krygier (2019: 761) has argued that even if the purpose of the rule of law could be answered in a number of different ways in the manner suggested here, 'the *distinctive* domain that has long been closely associated with the ideal of rule of law is the exercise of power'. See also his distinction between external rule of law purposes like economic development from the immanent hostility of the rule of law to arbitrary power: Krygier (2016a: 215–17).

[22] There are of course other examples of theories of the rule of law that reside within a larger philosophical project. John Rawls's (1971) consideration of the precepts of the rule of law articulated as part of his theory of distributive justice, with which we engage briefly in Section 2.2.2, is another.

commencement of this part. This oft-cited 'theory of' the rule of law belongs to the work of Albert Venn Dicey, the nineteenth-century theorist of the English constitution who is widely credited with popularising the term 'the rule of law' (Walters, 2020: 227–8). Three elements, or demands, are associated with it. The first is the demand that government proceed through a framework of legal norms and procedures rather than through unconstrained discretion. The second is the demand of equality between government officials and private individuals before the same ordinary law and the same ordinary courts.[23] The third is the establishment and protection of individual rights through the development of the judge-made common law (Walters, 2020: 228–30).

These three demands are frequently positioned as the starting point for understanding the meaning of the rule of law as an element of constitutionalism within the English tradition of constitutional thought and practice (Barber, 2018: 85–119). For our purposes, however, the point to notice is the specific context of those three demands (English constitutional practice as it stood in Dicey's time) and the specific motivation for articulating them (Dicey's desire to protect that constitutional system from decay). When this context is understood, it is clear that Dicey could not have intended his theory to be a general theory of the rule of law applicable to all times, places, and people – even if some of its demands, such as the equality of government officials and private individuals before the ordinary law – appear to be generalisable (Walters, 2021: 153–4).

Nonetheless, Dicey's theory of the rule of law has taken root in a range of contexts beyond that into which it was born and towards which it was aimed – to the strong lament of some.[24] Indeed, leading Dicey scholar Mark Walters (2021: 161) has suggested that the view of English society informing Dicey's thinking on the rule of law was an 'imaginary country' even in Dicey's own time. A much more extensive role for government – and thus also for legislated law as its mode of rule – had already begun to emerge through what came to be known as the 'administrative state'.

We need this last piece of context to understand the normative impulse behind this particular theory of the rule of law. Dicey 'bemoaned what he saw as a decline in respect for the Rule of Law in England', and was particularly troubled by the development in neighbouring France of a specific body of administrative law to regulate the actions of public officials (Waldron, 2016: 3.4). His famous objection to administrative discretion – to which we return in Section 3.2.2 – belongs here. As his equality demand makes clear, to Dicey's mind the rule of law (in England)

---

[23] For an in-depth treatment of what Dicey meant by ordinary, see Walters (2020: chs. 5 and 9).

[24] Joseph Raz, for example, complained that 'English writers have been mesmerized by Dicey's unfortunate doctrine for too long' (1979: 218), while the political theorist Judith Shklar famously described Dicey's theory as an 'unfortunate outburst of Anglo-Saxon parochialism' (1987: 5).

required that public officials and private individuals be subject to the same general laws and have their causes adjudicated in the same courts. When combined with his preoccupation with 'the security given under the English constitution to the rights of individuals' (Walters, 2020: 230), it is not difficult to see why Dicey's theory of the rule of law is regarded as a leading example of a negative conception of the rule of law specifically concerned with protecting private rights from the encroachments of government through the development of judge-made common law. We return to these ideas at multiple points in Part 2.

1.5.2 A Rule of Law Theory to Support Spontaneous Order

The third vignette with which we commenced this part is taken from (the first iteration of) Friedrich Hayek's theory of the rule of law. The similarities between that vignette and its neighbour, taken from Dicey, are hardly accidental: Hayek's embrace of the English (*Lex, Rex*) rule of law tradition was a reaction to and rejection of the logic of his native (*Rex, Lex*) *Rechtsstaat* tradition (Section 1.2.3). Because Hayek ultimately developed aspects of his thinking on the rule of law on three occasions,[25] pinning down his theory of the rule of law can be difficult beyond noticing his consistent preoccupation with five interconnected ideas.

The first is a negative conception of liberty, in the sense of *freedom from* the encroachments of government. The second is a preoccupation with 'spontaneous order', the implicit patterns of conduct that arise when individuals interact freely with each other, as compared to when their conduct is managed or coerced by government. The third is an emphasis on law as a framework of general and generally applicable rules that (at most) adjust rather than order these private interactions. The fourth is faith in the market as the crucial mechanism for the production of this spontaneous order. The fifth is an emphasis on courts and judges as the guardians of this spontaneous order through the incremental case-by-case method of the English the common law tradition (Section 2.4).[26]

The interactions between these five connected ideas in Hayek's thought can be complex,[27] and this complexity can be amplified by the often-polemical tone of his work as well as the theory of knowledge ultimately underscoring it. But with respect to what Hayek thought the rule of law should do – its function – one theme is recurrent. Even if *some* interference by government in the lives of individuals is inevitable,[28] the task of the rule of law is to provide the framework

---

[25] Hayek (2006, 2007, 2013).

[26] See especially Hayek (2013: 113). On the significance of courts and judges to Hayek's thought, see St-Hilaire and Baron (2019: 10–16).

[27] For an accessible overview of Hayek's legal thought, see Postema (2011).

[28] '[I]t is the character rather than the volume of government activity that is important', Hayek (2006: 194).

within which 'an individual can foresee the action of the state and make use of this knowledge as a datum in forming his own plans' (Hayek, 2007: 118).

As we also saw for Dicey, it is not possible to understand Hayek's thinking on the rule of law, in whichever iteration, without appreciating the historical and political context in which it was initially developed. Published in 1944, Hayek's most polemical work and the home of our third vignette, *The Road to Serfdom*, was a plea to not continue into peacetime the kind of economic planning that had increased the coercive role of government in the lives of individuals during wartime. Hayek's avowed opposition to the 'welfare state' in turn explains the close association that developed between his thought and the political philosophy of 'neoliberalism' that sees the role of government primarily in terms of facilitating conditions in which the market can take root as the central organising mechanism of social and political order (Section 2.6.1). Indeed, as Shklar (1987: 9) described it, Hayek's rule of law 'does far more than to make the citizen feel secure from the agents of coercive government': it was designed to sustain that 'spontaneous order' – the free market economy – that Hayek positioned as the foundation of all other aspects of society.

We return to the significance of the battle between neoliberalism and the welfare state to contemporary rule of law thought and practice in Section 2.6.1. The point for now is simply that Hayek's rule of law thought is not only a prime example of a 'theory within a theory' but also an optimal illustration of the importance of the context if we are to understand why a given theory of the rule of law has the content and carries the associations that it does.[29]

1.6 The Rule of Law and the Nature of Law

If the rule of law is the rule of *law*, it follows that there will always be a conception of law in play, or at stake, within any theory of the rule of law.

For many who work with the idea, squabbles about the conception of law informing a particular theory of the rule of law may seem of little consequence. But for others that conception is a crucial part of how and why they theorise the rule of law in the way they do. Philosophers of legal positivism have done the most to argue for a strict *dis*connection between the concept of 'law' on the one hand and the concept of 'the rule of law' on the other. To understand why, however, we need to become acquainted with (at least part of) the much more longstanding jurisprudential debate about the separability of 'law' on the one hand and 'morality' on the other.[30] The iteration of that debate of greatest significance to theoretical

---

[29] For reflections on the role of private law in rule of law thought, see Austin and Klimchuk (2014).

[30] Two other well-known twentieth century legal philosophers who integrated their thinking on law per se with their thinking on the rule of law are John Finnis (1980: 270–6), and Ronald Dworkin (see especially Dworkin (1986, 2004).

engagement with the rule of law is what became known as 'Hart–Fuller debate' (Fuller, 1958; Hart, 1958) in the mid-twentieth century.

The part of that debate of most relevance to present concerns arose from Fuller's analysis of what we earlier described as the 'formal' principles of the rule of law (Section 1.3.2). The point in dispute was whether these formal principles (in the guise of Account #1 reproduced in Section 1.3.2) must be observed in order for law itself to exist. Fuller had associated those formal demands with the morality side of the law and morality debate through his idea that law contained an internal morality, thus purportedly demonstrating positivism's error in insisting on the strict separability of the two.[31] Though Fuller himself did not refer to the principles of his 'internal morality of law' as principles of the rule of law,[32] Joseph Raz later decided that Fuller's position might be better read as challenging Hart to explain whether the 'formal' principles of the rule of law[33] were part of the concept of law defended by legal positivists. Thus, what Raz did in his seminal essay, 'The Rule of Law and Its Virtue' (Raz, 1979), was effectively to remodel the Hart–Fuller debate into one about the conceptual separability of law and the rule of law.

To do so, however, was not to escape the matters at issue within its original iteration. To win that original debate, Hart needed to defend the claim that nothing of a moral character gets mixed into positivism's account of what it means for law to exist. This demand carried over into the task Raz needed to overcome to defend the claim that law (also) does not require observance of the principles we associate with the rule of law in order to exist. To do so, Raz needed to demonstrate that any moral 'goods' (Section 2.2) that might attach to our understanding of the rule of law are separable from what makes law, law.

This was and is, by any measure, tricky philosophical territory. There is accordingly a certain irony to how Raz's 'The Rule of Law and Its Virtue' is regularly assigned as a foundational theoretical reading on the rule of law even though a deeper knowledge of longstanding debates in legal philosophy is required to navigate at least some aspects of its analysis. This is especially so in relation to two key features of that analysis. The first is the significance of Raz's presentation of the rule of law as an ideal (Section 1.2.4) to the argument about the conceptual separability of law and the rule of law that he sought to defend. The point here is that something that is no more than a contingently realised ideal (the rule of law) cannot be a *necessary* condition for something else (law). Some knowledge of the

---

[31] For an extended treatment of this debate, and of Fuller's idea of the internal morality of law specifically, see Rundle (2012: chs. 3–5, 2016) respectively.

[32] See Section 3.4 generally and footnote 71 specifically.

[33] Raz's own version of these principles, reproduced as Account #2 at Section 1.3.2, built on Fuller's original eight.

foundational commitments of legal positivism is also needed to grasp Raz's famous argument that the rule of law is the virtue of law like sharpness is the virtue of a knife (1979: 225). The message here is that observing the principles of the rule of law merely makes the instrument of law more effective in achieving the ends to which it is put, good or evil as those ends may be. If law is an amoral instrument, neutral as to the ends to which it might be put, then the rule of law as the instrumental virtue of law must also be morally neutral: its observance does no more than aid law's work, moral or immoral as that work might be. Advancing this argument thus ensures that the central tenet of legal positivism – that law and morality are necessarily separable – remains intact.[34]

When Raz revisited his analysis of the rule of law four decades later (Raz, 2019), none of these arguments were reopened. To Raz and other proponents of no more than an instrumental association between law and the rule of law (Gardner, 2012), the debate was settled in 1979. Others are less certain (Waldron, 2008: 11; Simmonds, 2010: 285; Rundle, 2013: 779–82). The point for our purposes is a much less contested one: namely, simply to point out that some of the most famous arguments about the rule of law in contemporary Anglo-American legal philosophy were never just about the rule of law. They were *also* a contribution to ongoing debates about the nature of law itself. So long as the idea of the rule of law is about the rule of *law*, questions about the nature of law will always be part of the picture, acknowledged or otherwise.

1.7 Getting Organised

The sheer scale of scholarship that engages with the idea of the rule of law is daunting. Efforts to map the field of rule of law theory by reference to some or other organising principle have accordingly become an academic enterprise in their own right, undertaken either for their own sake (St-Hilaire & Baron, 2019) or as a ground-clearing prelude to an engagement between the rule of law and another idea (Lacey, 2021).

There are many ways in which this organising exercise might be framed. The way that this part has been structured by reference to the different methods animating theoretical scholarship on the rule of law is one example of how the landscape of contemporary rule of law theory might be organised. The arrangement of the *Cambridge Companion to the Rule of Law* (Meierhenrich & Loughlin, 2021) into

---

[34] Raz makes two further arguments that (together with his sharp knife argument) are designed to defeat the claim that something of moral significance passes into law from its connection to the principles of the rule of law. The first is an argument about how only minimal compliance with these principles is needed for law to come into being. The second is an argument about how the rule of law is a negative virtue of law that stands to correct evils that only law can create (Raz, 1979: 223–4). For a close analysis of these arguments, see Rundle (2013).

contributions on the themes of histories, moralities, pathologies, and trajectories is another. The most common devices for organising rule of law theory are however the dichotomy (which divides engagements with the rule of law into two camps by reference to some organising theme or principle) and the taxonomy (which may have much larger organisational ambitions, but which again will be structured around particular organising themes or criteria).

The purpose of deploying either device is to illuminate certain features of particular ways of engaging theoretically with the rule of law. Yet as with all aspects of the latter enterprise, it is important to keep a critical eye on what such devices help us to see, and what they might, however inadvertently, conceal. A little more detail helps to make the point.

1.7.1 Dichotomies

The much-rehearsed distinction between 'formal' versus 'substantive', or 'thin' versus 'thick' theories of the rule of law has been for many years the 'go to' way of distinguishing one kind of rule of law theory from another. Both versions of the same distinction operate upon one particular feature of those theories: the demands that they make, or do not make, on the *content* of legal norms produced in purported compliance with the rule of law.

As we learned earlier (Section 1.3.1), a 'formal' rule of law theory only makes demands on the form that legal norms in a rule of law order must take. A 'substantive' theory of the rule of law is one that *also* includes demands on the substance, or content, of those legal norms. So understood, we can readily see the problem with situating the two within the binary of a dichotomy. Rather than being strictly opposed, a substantive theory of the rule of law might better be understood as a 'formal+' theory that takes a formal conception of the rule of law as its starting point, but then adds extra demands. As Pauline Westerman (2018: 141) has playfully described it, '[o]ne has to be thin in order to grow thick!'

The 'formal' versus 'substantive', or 'thin' versus 'thick' distinction is arguably the most well-worn dichotomy around which theories of the rule of law are organised because of the ease with which it can attach to the dominant method for theorising the rule of law: the provision of an account of its essential principles or features. As we saw in Section 1.3.2, the laundry list format helps to lay bare the formal, procedural and substantive characteristics of the principles claimed to be necessary to the rule of law. Yet as we also have seen, not all theories of the rule of law take the shape of a list, even if some are often absorbed into the received formal versus substantive binary regardless. Dicey's theory of the rule of law, for example, is often retrofitted into a formal theory, despite reservations from those most familiar with his project (Lino, 2018: 744; Walters, 2020: 234–45).

There are of course other ways in which the field of rule of law theory might be dichotomised. One recent example is an effort to map theories of the rule of law according to their explicit or implicit embrace of an idea of 'law as will' versus an idea of 'law as artificial reason' (St-Hilaire & Baron, 2019). The point to notice for present purposes is how this particular way of organising the field initiates engagement with an arguably wider range of works than might customarily be included in a formal versus substantive / thick versus thin organisation, precisely because it is not principally concerned with theoretical engagements directed to uncovering the necessary features of the rule of law.[35]

1.7.2 Taxonomies

The move towards more complex taxonomies through which to map theoretical scholarship on the rule of law might be the strongest sign that dichotomies of kind just reviewed may no longer be sufficiently serviceable to a field that has outgrown their binary parameters. Taxonomies of rule of law theory remain an exercise in distinguishing different types of theoretical endeavour from each other, but with a view to drawing distinctions rather than oppositions.

One illustration is that recently offered by Nicola Lacey (2021: 458–73) in her analysis of the rule of law and populism.[36] The point for present purposes is to notice why a taxonomical exercise was undertaken for an analysis of that kind. When a scholar seeks to engage one idea (such as the rule of law) with another (such as populism) the meaning of *both* needs to be clarified in order for any such engagement to be possible. In her effort to do precisely that clarificatory ground clearing on the rule of law side, Lacey (2021: 460–2) suggests that contemporary theoretical scholarship on the rule of law might be organised into four basic categories: formal/thin approaches, procedural approaches, substantive/thick approaches, and teleological/functional approaches.

The matter of interest for our purposes is not whether this is the right way to build a taxonomy of contemporary rule of law theory. The point is simply to notice how each category in this (or any other) taxonomy must attach itself to some feature of a particular theoretical approach that distinguishes it from others. Sometimes that feature will be the method through which a particular theoretical treatment of the rule of law is pursued, on other occasions the character of its content, and on other occasions something else again.

---

[35] St-Hilaire and Baron's 'law as will' versus 'law as artificial reason' dichotomy engages with works by Hobbes, Coke, Dicey, Hayek, Fuller, Hart, Raz, Dworkin, and Waldron.

[36] The title of this first part of our study, 'Approaching the Rule of Law', is borrowed from Lacey's (2021: 460) use of the same in relation to this taxonomical exercise.

1.8 Theories Revisited

It should by now be clear that there is no such thing as rule of law theory as a single enterprise, nor any single method through which that enterprise might be pursued. Rather, different theories of the rule of law have different reasons for coming into being, and different things to offer. They should always be read, interpreted, and applied with this in mind.

But when is a particular work a theory of the rule of law in any event? This question is especially salient to the contemporary life of the idea, in which a range of different people work with it in a range of different ways. Those who work on international rule of law promotion and measurement initiatives, for example, likely understand themselves as practitioners rather than theorists of the idea. Nonetheless, by giving definition to the idea for the purpose of its mobilisation in the world, these practitioners are also engaging in a kind of theoretical exercise.[37] From a very different angle, the rule of law entries to be found in recent perspective-seeking scholarly companion collections on subjects of legal and political thought might not be theories of the rule of law in their own right, but they are a particular style of scholarship about the idea – or about ideas about the idea – that warrant examination on their own terms.[38]

Recent years have also seen whole bodies of scholarship on the rule of law produced by particular scholars as leading interpreters of the thought of others or as theorists of the idea in their own right.[39] Jeremy Waldron's multifaceted treatment of the rule of law, for example, not only amounts to a canon of theoretical work on the idea but also yields a theory of the rule of law that is sensitive to institutions, emphasises the significance of procedures, elevates the importance of legislation and legislatures, orients to the value of dignity, and takes seriously connections between the rule of law and democracy.[40]

The point with which to conclude this part's study of *how* theories of the rule of law are pursued is accordingly a simple one. When approaching any such theory, it pays to keep in mind that by far the greatest influence on *how* theories of the rule of law are pursued will be the purposes of the scholar who sets out to do so – narrow or wide, explicit or implicit, as those purposes might be. Everything has its context.

---

[37] See, for example, the explanations given to the phrase 'the rule of law' by the United Nations, the International Monetary Fund, and the World Justice Project in footnotes 18–20.

[38] See, for example, Howarth (2015), Sajo (2019), and Tasioulas (2020).

[39] Here we might especially highlight scholarly works on the rule of law by David Dyzenhaus, Trevor Allan, Martin Krygier, William Scheuerman, and Brian Tamanaha, of which this Element engages with only a sample.

[40] See further Section 2.5.

2 Untangling the Rule of Law

2.1 Why Untangle?

Ideas travel together, they tend to travel in particular directions, and they invariably carry a lot of baggage. The rule of law is no different to any other idea in these respects. It has always been closely entangled with other ideas.

The aim of this part is to reflect on the implications of these entanglements for thinking about and working with the idea of the rule of law. Those considered here overlap in various ways, such that there is no straightforward way to address one without keeping in mind insights taken from another. Still, it is helpful to at least attempt to isolate the kinds of entanglements at issue within each, which for our purposes we will describe in terms of the contributions, companions, conflations, and controversies that travel with the idea of the rule of law.

2.2 Contributions

2.2.1 Packaging the Goods

Most engagements with the rule of law commence from the premise that it is a good thing, or at least that it does something good. The reason for this assumption goes back to the point emphasised at the beginning of Part 1. The rule of law is a particular way of organising political power, and one that has long been thought to protect against problems of tyranny and arbitrariness (Section 1.2.2). In its association with this protective or preventative contribution, the rule of law has long held a reputation for being a good thing.

As a subject of theoretical analysis, however, what the rule of law is thought to be good *for* is a separate question to what is thought to be good *about* it. Analytic philosophers cast this as a distinction between instrumental and intrinsic value. Arguments about the instrumental value of the rule of law concern its value to the achievement of some external end. We became acquainted with this kind of argument when we examined how philosophers of legal positivism defend a distinction between the concept of the rule of law and the concept of law as part of defending their foundational claim (the separability thesis) that there is no necessary connection between law and morality (Section 1.6). We can now see why an instrumental argument about what the rule of law is good for is so compatible with this enterprise. When Joseph Raz (1979: 225) argued that the rule of law is to law what sharpness is to a knife, its good-making quality, his point was that sharpness is the good-making quality of a knife regardless of whether the knife is used for good or bad ends. The same, Raz argued, applies to the rule of law as the good-making quality of law. It is an instrumental good, irrespective of whether legal ends supported by its observance are good or bad.

Instrumental arguments about the rule of law's contributions also abound in practice. For example, the United Nations' working definition of the rule of law makes a range of instrumental arguments about its contribution to various desirable states of affairs. There the rule of law is described as fundamental to 'international peace and security and political stability', achieving 'economic and social progress and development', the protection of 'people's rights and fundamental freedoms', as well as foundational to 'people's access to public services, curbing corruption, restraining the abuse of power, and to establishing the social contract between people and the state' (United Nations Secretary-General, 2004: 4).

Arguments about what is good about the rule of law are concerned with its intrinsic value: the good(s) thought to be inherent to the rule of law, as such. Arguments in this vein might include the claim that the rule of law is inherently compatible with the possession and experience of liberty (Section 2.2.2), or that legal procedures typically associated with the rule of law, such as the right to a fair trial, foster respect for dignity (Section 2.5.2). The idea behind such claims about intrinsic value is that to have the rule of law is to have these goods, as if the two simply come together.

The line between arguments about instrumental versus intrinsic value can sometimes be hard to draw clearly. The familiar claim that observance of the rule of law contributes to the legitimacy of political rule (Section 2.2.3) for example, could plausibly be classified as either an instrumental argument about what the rule of law is good for, or as an argument about what is intrinsically good about it. For the less philosophically initiated, simply identifying that a particular theoretical engagement with the rule of law (or part thereof) is concerned with the contribution(s) of the rule of law is likely to be more important than determining whether the relevant analysis is best classified as concerned with its instrumental or intrinsic value. Indeed, because much of rule of law thought simply takes it as given that the rule of law is a good thing, the more likely focus of engagements oriented to the contributions of the rule of law will be with *why* we should value it.[41] Two examples help to illustrate.

2.2.2 Liberty

The term 'liberty is generally understood to denote the particular species of freedom that is possessed and experienced within a political order.[42] The question of how to foster conditions for liberty has always been the central preoccupation of inquiry into the political dimensions of the rule of law.

---

[41] We address arguments for why we should *not* value the rule of law in Section 2.6.

[42] Liberty so understood is to be distinguished from freedom, which is thought to attach to the natural state of human beings rather than to their status within a political order.

Indeed, it is generally safe to assume that all theoretical engagements with the rule of law have at least some concern, explicitly or implicitly, for its asserted contribution to liberty.

What *kind* of liberty is associated with observance of the rule of law is, however, another question (Allan, 2013: 89). As we emphasised in Part 1 (Sections 1.1 and 1.2.2), the dominant orthodoxy of rule of law thought is cast in negative terms. A particular perspective on liberty is central to this orthodoxy: liberty is that which subjects of the rule of law possess, and experience, in the spaces where law is *not*.[43] There are however more positive ways of thinking about liberty in relation to the rule of law, and which open up the potential for a connection with the presence rather than the absence of law. We return to these arguments in Section 2.6.

In our treatment of the claimed distinction between the rule of law and rule by law (Section 1.2.3), we noted that something of great import must consist in the 'of' of the rule of law that is absent in the 'by' of rule by law. That difference was explained in terms of the direction of legal obligations: it is only the rule of law that is associated with an idea of reciprocal constraint, where ruler and ruled alike are mutually subordinate to law. But on its own, this demand of mutual subordination tells us little about *how* the rule of law contributes to the liberty of subjects within a political order so committed.

Theorists of the rule of law disagree on this point, but for present purposes, we can learn from an example of how a conception of liberty informs larger arguments of political thought within which the rule of law is assigned an important place. The twentieth-century political philosopher, John Rawls (1971), positioned liberty at the centre of his development and defence of principles of distributive justice. To do so, however, he needed to explain what idea of liberty he had in mind. Rawls (1971: 239) articulated an idea of liberty as 'a complex of rights and duties defined by institutions', and argued that the rule of law contributes to liberty so understood through how its 'regularities' (the security of knowing what to expect of those who make and enforce rules) create 'the boundaries of men's liberties' (Rawls, 1971: 235, 239). Rawls then further contended that the rule of law makes this specific contribution to liberty through formal precepts, which he called 'justice as regularity', that concern 'the impartial and regular administration of rules' (1971: 235, 236).

This is just one set of interconnected arguments that articulate a worked-out view about the contribution of the rule of law to liberty. What matters for our

---

[43] See, for example, Friedrich Hayek's (2006: 182) classic statement of this position: 'What distinguishes a free from an unfree society is that in the former each individual has a recognized private sphere clearly distinct from the public sphere, and the private individual cannot be ordered about but is expected to obey only the rules which are equally applicable to all'.

purposes, above all, is simply to be aware that just as there will always be a conception of law in play or at stake in a given theory of the rule of law (Section 1.6), there will also always be a conception of liberty in play or at stake within any discussion of the claimed contribution of the rule of law to this most exalted of human ends.

2.2.3 Legitimacy

Bound up with its claimed contributions to fostering conditions for liberty is the association between the rule of law and the legitimacy of political rule. We again need to return to the rule of law's political demand of mutual subordination to law to understand why.

Put at its simplest, the legitimacy argument has two limbs. The first is that the commitment of the ruler (and not just the ruled) to being governed by law is a way of showing respect for the ruled as autonomous individuals who have an interest in their liberty. The second limb of the argument is that, because of this commitment and the respect for liberty it entails, those ruled within a political order committed to the rule of law are more likely to regard such rule as legitimate. They are more likely to accept its authority over them.

The question of legitimacy is thus centrally concerned with why political authority can be acceptable to and accepted by those who are subject to it, from their perspective.[44] We can again gain insight into this dimension of rule of law thought by returning to the claimed distinction between the rule of law and rule by law (Section 1.2.3). The reason why the rule of law is thought to contribute to the perceived legitimacy of political rule conducted this way is because it is thought to offer *something more* to those subject to such rule than bare legality understood as power authorised through the instrument of law (Dyzenhaus, 2022: 88–148). We can now see how the question of *what* this 'something more' is loops us back to arguments about the contribution of the rule of law to liberty. But, having arrived back there, we return to the question of what kind of liberty it is, and how it comes to manifest.

On this point we can gain illumination from the more sophisticated and historically situated distinction between the rule of law and *Rechtsstaat* political traditions. As we learned in Section 1.2.3, law is assigned a different role within each: in the rule of law, tradition law is understood as a constraint on political power (*Lex, Rex*), while in the *Rechtsstaat* tradition law is understood as a conduit of political power (*Rex, Lex*). The point of interest for present purposes is how the different role assigned to law within each travels alongside a distinction between individual and political liberty and the relationship

---

[44] See further Section 3.3.1.

between them. In the *Rechtsstaat* tradition, political liberty – the liberty to participate in politics and thus to influence the values of a political order – is considered prior to individual liberty. On this view, individual liberty is thought best secured by first securing political liberty. In the rule of law tradition, the relationship runs in the other direction. Consistent with the idea that individual liberty is to be found in the spaces where law is *not*, the suggestion is that we need to secure conditions for individual liberty before we can secure political liberty. Meierhenrich's observation that the key difference between the *Rechtsstaat* (European) tradition and the rule of law (English) tradition 'has to do with the question of where the rights of individuals originate' is apposite. So too is his observation that the rule of law tradition has long been preoccupied with the legitimacy of law in ways that the *Rechtsstaat* tradition has not (Meierhenrich, 2021: 62, 64).

The key takeaway is accordingly this. If we understand individual liberty as the political endgame of the rule of law tradition, it follows that the legitimacy of any arrangement of political rule that lays claim to the rule of law must demonstrate how it is consistent with the individual liberty of those who are subject to it.

2.3 Companions

There are a number of reasons why inquiry into the rule of law might investigate its relation to another idea. Such an exercise might, for example, be pursued to distinguish the rule of law from that other idea, or to focus on their common elements. This kind of inquiry is different to the phenomenon with which we are concerned in this section, where the rule of law is placed in the close company of another idea as if they logically belong together. Companionships of this kind typically see the rule of law paired with a range of ideas associated with liberal political morality, such as human rights, democracy, and economic security, as if together they speak a common language.

The messages conveyed by such pairings, however, can be quite different from each other. If the rule of law is paired with democracy, for example, the message will likely have something to do with its contribution to the ability of individuals to participate in politics and thus to shape the commitments of their political order. If the rule of law is paired with economic security, the message will likely be about how the rule of law protects private property rights or is otherwise vital to a well-functioning economy. These are two quite different stories about the rule of law.

Our question, therefore, is this. In what ways might our understanding of the rule of law be shaped by its close association with other ideas?

2.3.1 The Stakes of Companionship

We noted in Part 1 that those who analyse the rule of law as a 'concept' seek to draw sharp distinctions between it and other concepts (Section 1.3). The aim, in essence, is to ensure that the rule of law and nothing but the rule of law is the object of analysis.

No one did more for this analytical cause than the philosopher Joseph Raz. In his first renowned analysis of the rule of law (Raz, 1979: 211), Raz argued that it 'is just one of the virtues that a legal system might possess and by which it might be judged', and 'is not to be confused with democracy, justice, equality (before the law or otherwise), human rights of any kind or respect for persons or for the dignity of man'. Putting the objection at its strongest, Raz (1979: 211) insisted that 'if the rule of law is the rule of the good law then to explain its nature is to propound a complete social philosophy'.

Raz (2019) elaborated this objection further in his last philosophical engagement with the rule of law, but in that instance with his eye on the common companionship between the rule of law and human rights specifically. The provocation to do so came from the writings of Tom Bingham (2010), the late British judge renowned for giving human rights protections a central place within his thinking on the rule of law. We encountered both Raz's and Bingham's accounts of the principles of the rule of law in Section 1.3.2, in association with formal and substantive conceptions of the rule of law, respectively. The point presently is that Bingham (2010: 67) advocated for a close companionship between the rule of law and human rights on the basis either that the two share essentially the same rationale, or are otherwise inseparable in practice.

Raz's response to Bingham offers a helpful prism through which to reflect on the stakes of encouraging or discouraging close companionship between the rule of law and other ostensibly compatible ideals or practices. In Raz's view nothing was achieved 'and much is lost' by simply grouping such ideals and practices together 'as though they share a rationale or are of similar importance, or are otherwise alike'. Clarity in theory and practice, he insisted, 'is achieved in recognising their diversity' (Raz, 2019: 10). The worry here is not just about analytical precision. As Jeremy Waldron has put the point, if the rule of law is used as 'a general stand-in for everything good one could ever want from a political system', we might lose sight of what is at stake in *different* legal and political goals, values, and tools (Waldron, 2021: 124). We can thus see the connections between a concern for the stakes of such companionships and the contributions, or goods, of the rule of law (Section 2.2).

Like all contests of rule of law thought, this one ultimately comes down to argument. What matters for the newcomer is simply to notice when companionships of this kind are in play, and to reflect on how and why they might shape the understanding of the rule of law presented in the relevant analysis. Our next discussion demonstrates just how varied these influences can be.

2.3.2 Companions on a Mission

Placing the rule of law in close companionship with other ideas is now such a common practice that, beyond academic writings, it is rare to see our protagonist travelling alone. This is especially so in the work of international organisations engaged in the work of international rule of law promotion (Chalmers & Pahuja, 2021; Humphreys, 2021: 476), though this is by no means the only setting. Everywhere we see the rule of law assigned a place among other ostensibly laudable goals or urgent needs, from the protection of human rights to the attainment of global peace and much besides.

Such companionships are now so ubiquitous that they are sometimes assigned the label 'rule of law discourse'. This is instructive. If the rule of law is only one idea among several within such discourse, why is it given the leading role? And why has this discourse developed anyway? Answering these questions demands inquiry into how and in what ways assigning the rule of law that role contributes to the justificatory dimensions of political practices associated with it. The rule of law's reputation for being a good thing (Section 2.2) is surely a big part of this picture. But as we take further elsewhere (Sections 2.5.2, 3.4.1, and 3.5), good for what, or for whom?

Our aim here is not to pass judgement on whether the discursive companionships contained within different instances of rule of law discourse are right or wrong in their content or assembly, but rather simply to encourage attention to how these companionships work, and to the work they appear to be doing. One especially generative example is the 'Declaration of the High-level Meeting of the General Assembly on the Rule of Law at the National and International Levels' adopted in 2012 by the United Nations General Assembly. Each of the forty-two paragraphs of that Declaration speaks to how commitment to the rule of law informs different aspects of the 'three pillars' of peace and security, development, and human rights said to define the UN's organisational mission. Together with an additional report (United Nations, 2014) commissioned to specify precisely how the rule of law relates to and furthers each of those three pillars, these documents effectively re-describe the overarching mission of the UN in terms of the mission of the rule of law.

Liora Lazarus's analysis (2018) of securitisation within rule of law discourse draws our attention to something different again. Based on an extensive study of domestic and international examples, Lazarus (2018: 1) contends that the rule of law 'is shifting paradigmatically from a concept embodying the limitation of the coercive state, to one integral to maintenance of law, order and security'. Moreover, the pattern over time has been one in which security appears to have become the leading idea, despite the relevant discourse ostensibly being about the rule of law. Lazarus's study thus highlights the conceptual distortions that can follow when the rule of law is placed in close companionship with another idea.

It is instructive to put Lazarus's analysis alongside the UN Declaration on the rule of law because both examples provoke us to ask where an association between the rule of law and another idea might end and an entire re-conceptualisation of the rule of law might begin. It is one thing to accept that the rule of law is an 'essentially contested concept' (Section 1.2.5). But might it be another altogether to stretch the idea in forty-two possible directions, or to swallow it within an agenda that is difficult to reconcile with its foundational political concern for the conditions necessary for liberty?

2.4 Connections

An orientation to the work of courts and judges is another connection that has proven so prevalent in modern thinking about the rule of law that it can be hard sometimes to detect where one idea ends and the other begins.[45] The first point to recall here is the longstanding association between the traditional 'negative' conception of the rule of law and courts, emphasised in our treatment of A. V. Dicey's (Section 1.5.1) and Friedrich Hayek's (Section 1.5.2) theories of the rule of law respectively. Courts in both projects are positioned as the guardians of the individual rights protected by the rule of law.

We should however be careful not to assume that all conceptions of the rule of law position courts and judges at their centre for the same reasons, or indeed share the same ideas about what, precisely, courts protect in the name of the rule of law. Montesquieu's model of the separation of powers (Section 2.5.1), for example, was motivated by a concern to ensure the existence of an independent judiciary that could protect the ruled against the aggressions of those who rule (Shklar, 1987: 4). By contrast in Hayek-influenced conceptions of the rule of law, the primary significance of courts lies in the availability of effective judicial enforcement of contractual and property rights against the encroachments of an

---

[45] The complexity of this connection can be amplified by how analyses of the relation of courts to the rule of law regularly borrow from or are informed by arguments drawn from related fields of theoretical endeavour, such as general legal theory, and constitutional theory. The legal philosophy debate between Ronald Dworkin (1977) and H. L. A. Hart (1961) is one example of the former, examining the role of courts in producing law, and how they do so. The longstanding debate in constitutional theory about whether courts or legislatures ought to have the last word on what is considered legal within a given constitutional system is an example of the latter: see Section 2.5.1.

overreaching state (Section 1.5.2). Certainly, both state-sanctioned violence and unreliable enforcement of contractual rights qualify as species of the kind of arbitrary power (Section 1.2.2) with which the rule of law tradition has been historically concerned. Each is, however, quite different in terms of *what* the presence of independent and well-functioning courts is thought to protect against, as well as in relation to *who* is likely to suffer, and in what ways, in the absence of such protection.[46]

Courts and judges can also be brought to the foreground of rule of law thought in engagements that attend closely to the tradition's particular institutional history. Waldron's examination (2012c) of the doctrine of precedent (or stare decisis) around which the English common law tradition of judge-made lawmaking is organised is an example. The perceived close association between the rule of law and the work of judges has however sometimes prompted the retort that if judges make law (as is unapologetically the case in the common law tradition) is this not a particular kind of 'rule of men'? Moreover, if judges make law, how can it be said that they, as the paragon rule of law officials, are also constrained by it? Emphasis on the particular comportment and abilities required of judges is a key feature of how rule of law theorists have responded to this retort (Section 3.3.2). Hayek (Section 1.5.2), however, took this point much further, positioning common law courts and judges as guardians and stewards of 'spontaneous order', serving, maintaining and improving 'a going order which nobody has designed' and 'that is not based on the individuals doing anybody's will' (Hayek, 2013: 113).

A more provocative question is to ask what might be lost to rule of law thought through its recurrent emphasis on courts and judges. The political theorist Judith Shklar (1987) was sharply critical of the extent to which modern rule of law theory focused on courts to (in her view) the neglect of the idea's historical context and political purpose. Not known for pulling her punches, Shklar (1987: 3) laid the blame for this development squarely at the feet of legal theorists who, she thought, 'tended to ignore every political reality outside the courtroom'. While this criticism applies primarily to *where* the gaze of contemporary rule of law theory has been directed, it equally encompasses questions about whether and in what circumstances the work of courts and judges reduces fundamental questions of politics into more tightly circumscribed questions of law, and what might be lost through this move.

A final general observation worth making about judges specifically in relation to the rule of law is that they are invariably among its theorists. Although judges will sometimes borrow a rule of law theory from one of its well-known

---

[46] We revisit this question in Section 3.4.1.

proponents (Fuller and Dicey have been especially popular on this front)[47] to support a particular line of judicial reasoning, at other times judges devise their own definitions or descriptions of the rule of law for the same end.[48] Judges necessarily engage in the business of theorising the rule of law, in jurisdiction-specific ways as well as in general terms, irrespective of whether they understand themselves as doing so when they do.

We return to the centrality of judges in rule of law thought in our attention to the officials of the rule of law in Section 3.3.2. What follows is a brief survey of two dominant themes of contemporary rule of law theory that connect, in some foundational way, to the work of courts and judges: claims made about the importance to the rule of law of procedure, and related claims about its connections to dignity.

2.4.1 Procedure

We are now well familiar with the idea that formal accounts of the rule of law make demands on the form that legal norms should take in a political order committed to the rule of law (Section 1.3.1). The demand that law in a condition of the rule of law consist of rules made publicly available is an example. These formal demands, however, say nothing about how those rules are applied. This is where the procedural dimensions of rule of law theory enter the picture. The concern here is with *how* law in a rule of law order is administered.

Why incorporate consideration of the rule of law's procedural dimensions within a discussion about its connection to courts? Even the briefest acquaintance with some of the typical procedural demands associated with the rule of law – such as the requirement that rules be applied impartially, or the requirement that a person accused of a wrong be given an opportunity to be heard on the point[49] – soon reveals that the procedural demands of the rule of law align closely with the kinds of processes associated with, and comportments expected of, courts and judges specifically. We might say that the conduct of courts and the behaviour of judges have historically provided the model for theorising these procedural demands. But there is more that pushes rule of law theory towards courts than this. If we recall that the core political demand of the rule of law is the idea that rulers and ruled alike are mutually subordinate to law, then it

---

[47] See, for example, *Palmer* v. *Western Australia* [2021] HCA 31, [22], [23].

[48] See, for example, *A (FC) and others (FC) (Appellants)* v. *Secretary of State for the Home Department (Respondent)* [2004] UKHL 56, [42], [74]; *R (Guardian News and Media Ltd)* v. *City of Westminster Magistrates' Court (Article 19 intervening)* [2012] EWCA Civ 420; [2013] QB 618, [1].

[49] For one discussion of the procedural dimensions of dispute resolution as an aspect of rule of law thought, see Bingham (2010: 85–109).

follows that the rule of law must also provide an opportunity for the (impartial) application of rules to be contested. Procedures are accordingly thought to be crucial not just for providing a framework for the application of law per se, but for the work of the rule of law as an argumentative practice.

Fleshing out this and other aspects of the rule of law's procedural dimensions has been one of the significant contributions made to contemporary rule of law theory by the philosopher Jeremy Waldron (2008, 2011, 2012b). Within that contribution, Waldron has especially emphasised the opportunities for voice and agency on the part of the subjects of a political order that lays claim to commitment to the rule of law that are offered by procedures. As he has put the point, the procedural side of the rule of law presents a mode of governance that allows people 'a way of intervening on their own behalf in confrontations with power' (Waldron, 2008: 8). Moreover, Waldron contends, it is through its procedural demands that the rule of law 'condemns official behaviour that treats individual agency as something of no consequence' (Waldron, 2008: 9). Of particular significance for our purposes is how by illuminating how procedures provide a vehicle through which subjects may make procedural demands on official conduct, Waldron brings the political dimensions of the rule of law into view. This resonates strongly with the analysis developed in Section 3.3.3 on thinking relationally about the rule of law.

2.4.2 Dignity

The invitation to attend to the circumstances of the legal subject that opens up through a focus on the rule of law's procedural dimensions has also generated arguments about its connections to dignity (Waldron, 2011: 16).[50] Here Waldron's thinking is inspired by Lon Fuller's jurisprudence, to which we also return in Section 3.3.3, and specifically the suggestion that departures from the eight principles associated with Fuller's account of the rule of law (Section 1.3.2) are 'an affront to man's dignity as a responsible agent' (Fuller, 1969: 163).

In developing this suggestion into a proposition of rule of law theory, Waldron (2012a: 201) describes dignity as a 'status concept' that has to do with the standing that a person has in society and in her dealings with others. The contribution of procedures to constituting that standing is not hard to see. If law is 'a mode of governing people that acknowledges that they have a view or perspective of their own to present on the application of the norm to their conduct and situation' (Waldron, 2012a: 210), then the rule of law must provide the channels through which this acknowledgment can be expressed.

---

[50] There are of course also general legal theory claims that can be made about the connections between law per se and dignity: see, for example, Waldron (2012a: 200–8) and Sempill (2018).

Hence Waldron's conclusion (2011: 16) that procedures embody 'a crucial dignitarian idea–respecting the dignity of those to whom the norms are applied as being capable of explaining themselves'.

Waldron's dignity analysis is raised here because it is closely tied to the work of courts, and specifically to the idea of the rule of law as an argumentative practice. We might ask, however, whether tethering the procedural demands of the rule of law primarily to patterns of practice typically adopted by courts sufficiently grasps the significance of procedure in the full range of institutional settings within which relationships between ruler and ruled arise. We might ask the same question of the associated emphasis on dignity. Jennifer Nedelsky (2011: 141) has observed that in the context of state-subject relations in the (non-judicial) sphere of the administrative state, not all of the relations that express dignity will foster abilities that are crucial to a subject's standing in relation to power, among which she includes abilities of 'perception, competence, judgment and capacity to act'. Nedelsky's provocation is that once we shift the institutional setting, it could be that we need more than dignitarian arguments to illuminate the significance of procedural protections to the rule of law's core political demand of mutual subordination of ruler and ruled alike to the law. We return to these questions in Sections 3.3 and 3.4.

2.5 Conflations

The rule of law is so often associated with constitutionalism that the two ideas regularly risk being conflated with one another. The project of constitutionalism concerns particular institutional arrangements for organising and limiting the activity of government through law. Which is to say, constitutionalism might be understood as a particular way of doing the rule of law.

This does not however explain the precise character of the relation between the two. For some, the rule of law is the leading 'principle' of constitutionalism (Allan, 2001, 2013), while for others the rule of law is no more than one of its animating but unenforceable 'values' (Crawford, 2017). Those who engage the two ideas will each have their reasons for describing their relation in particular ways. Our objective here is not to resolve these finer distinctions of constitutional theory, but to direct attention to how the idea of the rule of law figures within scholarly engagement with constitutionalism. We have addressed one of the institutions of a constitutional order – the judiciary – in the study just undertaken of the rule of law and courts. We begin here, therefore, with the idea that goes to the heart of modern constitutionalism and which is itself closely aligned with the idea of the rule of law: the separation of powers.

2.5.1 The Separation of Powers

It is usually the eighteenth century French political theorist, Montesquieu (2001), who is credited for devising the model of the constitutional separation of legislative, executive, and judicial power. The basic thought behind the model is that within a given political order each kind of power is distinct and should be separated from the other two. Translating this theory to practice, the idea is that the institutional embodiments of these three different kinds of power – legislatures, executive branch entities, and courts – should each have a clear domain of operation that is functionally separate from the other two.

When the separation of powers is understood as a model of government aimed at limiting power, as well as providing mechanisms for calling such power to account, it is not difficult to see why it is sometimes suggested that the rule of law and the separation of powers are basically the same thing. There is however much more that needs to be thought through than this casual conflation allows (Waldron, 2013).[51] On its own, the idea of the separation of powers tells us little about *how* the power of each branch of a constitutional order is constrained in relation to the other, or how conflicts between the branches are best resolved. It also tells us little about what role law plays in enforcing such hierarchies and what kinds of law play that role. Indeed, among the most resilient debates in contemporary constitutional theory concerns which branch – legislature or judiciary – should have the final say about what is valid and enforceable law within a given constitutional system.[52] The precise character of the relation thought to hold between the rule of law and the separation of powers will obviously also depend on which conception of the rule of law is in play in that evaluation (Bellamy, 2005).

2.5.2 Legislatures

As we examine more closely in Section 3.2.1, the legal form usually presumed to be operating within rule of law thought is enacted general rules. This is, however, not always what is in view when the idea is put in conversation with the constitutional institution of the legislature specifically. When that conversation arises, it usually does so in connection with one of two primarily political stories. The first is a story about the assumed character of the political system

---

[51] See generally Waldron's (2013) analysis of these questions, and his argument that the two ideas share a rationale of articulated governance, where Waldron also addresses the argumentative work to be done to make the connection between the separation of powers and liberty: Waldron (2013: 454).

[52] Constitutional theorists often refer to this debate as a contest between theories of political constitutionalism (where the legislature gets the final say) and legal constitutionalism (where the judiciary gets the final say): see especially Allan (2001, 2013) and Bellamy (2009).

that engages in the enactment of legislation – representative democracy – and its relationship to the rule of law. The second is a story about the political agenda in play when such a representative democracy engages in the activity of legislating. Both stories warrant brief examination here to demonstrate why, when we see the idea of the rule of law placed in connection with legislatures and legislation, we need to step back and observe how and why that connection is being made.

We have said little so far about the claimed connections between the rule of law and democracy. In our examination of the rule of law's companions (Section 2.3.2), we noted that democracy is frequently among the cluster of laudable ideals and practices that appear within 'rule of law discourse'. We return to these companionships, but from a more critical perspective, in Section 2.6.1. Our concern for present purposes is that despite what appears to be indicated in this oft-seen companionship, the association between the rule of law and democracy is a site of controversy within rule of law thought (Hutchinson, 1999; Gargarella, 2021; Krygier, 2021) that has close connections to associations between the rule of law and constitutionalism. Contests of rule of law thought that centre upon the proper role for legislatures will very often (also) be informed by an underlying story about the proper role for democracy in a political order committed to the rule of law.

Grasping these institutional and political undercurrents is equally important for understanding the second story about the political agenda thought (by some) to be reflected in the activity of legislating. To illuminate what is going on here, we need to return to the perceived intimate relationship between the rule of law and the courts discussed in Section 2.4, as well as the perceived tensions between the idea of the rule of law and political objectives associated with the 'welfare state'. We investigate these tensions further in Section 2.6, but for present purposes we can get a sense of the issues in play by considering the stance taken *against* the role of legislatures and legislation in Friedrich Hayek's treatment of the rule of law (Section 1.5.2).

Like Dicey before him (Section 1.5.1), Hayek's pushback against legislation in association with the rule of law was not about legislation per se. It was about the political agenda he thought to be pursued (and the 'will' coercively imposed on individuals) when legislatures legislate to appropriate private wealth to fund social and collective causes. On this logic, the problem with democratically elected legislatures lies in how they are positioned to take (private law recognised) property away from its (private law protected) owners through the imposed will of enacted (public) law. The virtue of courts, by contrast, is that they exist to protect and enforce such private legal rights against such encroachments by the state (Sections 1.5.2 and 2.4).

This is a very simplified picture: Hayek's thought on legislatures, legislation, courts and the rule of law developed over the course of his writings on the subject.[53] The rule of law analyses of those sympathetic to Hayek's work also contains a range of nuanced positions that enrich our understanding of the idea (Allan, 2014; St-Hilaire & Baron, 2019). The point for present purposes is simply that once we peel back the layers, we will often see that arguments *against* legislation and legislatures pitched in a rule of law register are very often arguments *for* courts and their role in protecting individual rights, particularly private property rights. Similarly – but in reverse – arguments for legislatures pitched in a rule of law register are often likely to be arguments in favour of an at best *limited* role for courts in protecting private property rights against democratically mandated redistribution of wealth through legislation (Waldron, 2007, 2012b).

Yet as we will see in Section 2.6, for some the ideological tendencies of contemporary rule of law discourse and practice are so hardwired towards the protection of private property rights as to foster no plausible alignment with a strong participatory democracy committed to redistributing private wealth to social and collective causes through force of legislation. Historical attitudes towards legislatures and legislation are more complex. Dicey, for example, was a strong supporter of parliamentary sovereignty as a core principle – along with the rule of law – of English constitutionalism. Yet he also railed against the rising tide of late nineteenth-century political collectivism that he thought was seeing the law of England '"officialised" ... by statutes passed under the influence of socialistic ideas' (Dicey, 1915: 150; Loughlin, 1992: 153–9).

The crucial takeaway, then, is that engagements between the rule of law and legislatures are rarely about either idea in the abstract. They are more likely to be about advancing or deflecting ideologically laden background contests about what the rule of law is meant to do, how, and for whom.

2.5.3 The Executive Branch

On the one hand, the rule of law analysis of the executive branch is straightforward: it is here, after all, that we encounter the fundamental preoccupation of the former with power held by political entities with authority to govern. The executive branch of a constitutional system is the government within that system. Its actors and activities lie at the very heart of rule of law thought.

On the other hand, the rule of law analysis of the executive branch can be immensely complex. For a start, it is often difficult to work out who or what the executive branch is. While the legislative branch of a constitutional order is institutionally associated with legislatures, and the judicial branch with courts,

---

[53] Hayek (2006, 2007, 2013).

any number of institutions might comprise what we know as the executive branch. These may range from the office of the president or of a constitutional monarch, to ministers of government in the Westminster model, to government agencies or bureaucracies, administrative decision-making tribunals, and private service providers contracted to perform the functions of government.[54] Who or what is the executive is a question that has been answered differently in different constitutional systems and at different points in history, and there is every reason to think it will continue to be.

Our aims here, therefore, are necessarily modest: to no more than trace out some of the key questions associated with analyses of actors and activities of the executive branch that are customarily framed in a rule of law register.

Constraining the Executive

As we learned in Section 2.4.1, the doctrine of the separation of powers embodies the fundamental commitment of liberal constitutionalism to the dispersal rather than concentration of power. We can take two key messages from this for present purposes. The first is that the executive is only one of the branches of a constitutional order and should not be dominant over the others. The second is that the power of the executive branch should not be unduly concentrated.

In relation to the first point, the idea of the rule of law is commonly thought to be exemplified in the mechanism of judicial review:[55] the activity of subjecting executive action to the scrutiny and remedial powers of courts to ensure that it remains within the boundaries of what has been prescribed by law. As for the idea that the power of the executive branch should not be unduly concentrated, here the institutional relationships get much more complex for the fact that a considerable amount of work to counter the concentration of executive power is done through entities of the executive branch itself. This challenges the logic of the classic separation of powers model (Ackerman, 2000; McMillan, 2010) at the same time as it brings the conceptual and practical puzzles involved in determining who and what comprise the executive branch into relief. Kate Glover Berger's observation (2016: 158) that the structural character of the rule of law in contemporary constitutional conditions appears to be 'flattening'

---

[54] See further Section 3.3.2.

[55] The term here is to be distinguished from the use of the same to describe judicial invalidation of legislative action. There is a vast literature with which we do not deal here, especially in the United States, which addresses a 'rule of judges' objection to judicial review of legislation on the basis of the democratic legitimacy of enacted laws. Though related in some key respects, the specific ideological debate about legislation in connection with the rule of law noted at Section 2.2 can be distinguished from this more general democratic objection to judicial review of legislation.

is a comment on the complex character of the contemporary executive branch as much as it is a comment on its relation to the idea of the rule of law.

Emergencies

Nothing brings commitments into relief better than a crisis. This is never truer than when a declared 'emergency' shifts the locus of power within a constitutional order to the executive branch. At its most extreme, government in times of emergency might involve the suspension of all 'normal' legislatively enacted or judicially created law to which actors of the executive branch are ordinarily subordinate. Emergencies introduce conceptual puzzles into rule of law thought precisely because the role of law in times of emergency is thought to exemplify rule by law rather than the rule of law (Section 1.2.3) for the reason that emergencies ostensibly permit a concentration of power in the executive branch and limited supervision of such power by the legislative and judicial branches.

Those who rally in the name of the rule of law against the very idea of 'emergency government' thus make a very particular demand (Dyzenhaus, 2008). Their argument is that meaningful observance of the rule of law must hold in normal and emergency conditions alike. Or, at the very least, practice on the ground must pull more towards the rule of law end of the spectrum than the rule by law end. What warrants emphasis for present purposes is that even if that demand is levelled, above all, at the executive, its translation to the legislative and judicial branches is equally crucial. Put at its simplest, people only have as much power as they are given. The power of the executive branch, in emergency and normal times alike, is ultimately a product of how the other two branches conceive of their own roles and responsibilities in relation to that power.

A subplot of the rule of law dilemmas associated with emergencies is sometimes described as the problem of weaponising the rule of law, or among constitutional scholars, as 'abusive' or 'authoritarian' constitutionalism (Ginsburg & Moustafa, 2008; Dixon & Landau, 2021). Whether set against a backdrop of declared emergency, or other conditions that depart from liberal commitments ordinarily associated with constitutionalism, the worry here is about formal indicators of the rule of law manifesting in arrangements that otherwise have no commitment to the project of subordinating rulers and ruled alike to the demands of law.[56] Unsurprisingly, whether expressed in a rule of law or a constitutional register, discussion of such practices usually loops back to a conversation about legitimacy (Section 2.2.3).

---

[56] Stacking courts with judges who are politically sympathetic to authoritarian rather than democratic modes of rule is another practice often analysed in a rule of law register.

Philosophy of Law

The Executive as Lawmaker

There is another set of questions to be asked about whether the rule of law is threatened when the executive, rather than the legislature or judiciary, is the lawmaker. The kinds of executive law ostensibly tolerated in a rule of law order are notorious for being difficult to pin down, as the fluid boundaries of the common law 'prerogative' amply illustrate (Poole, 2010). The question for present purposes, however, concerns might be at stake, rule of law-wise, in executive lawmaking.

The different forms of law that comprise the output of this activity – delegated legislation, regulations, by-laws, directions and decrees, amongst others – pass the test of legal pedigree in the sense that they are the product of recognised lawgiving institutions within the system in which they are made (Hart, 1961). The political pedigree of such laws however is usually more dubious: after all, the primary lawmaking institution within a democratic constitutional order is meant to be the elected legislature. Grappling with executive lawmaking in a rule of law register, however, requires awareness of more than matters of legal and political pedigree. It demands a more specific set of questions about its purposes, character, and extent. When doing no more than giving effect to a legislative programme by filling in details or applying special expertise, executive lawmaking can be relatively uncontroversial in rule of law terms (Sunstein & Vermeule, 2018). But if such lawmaking is so wide-ranging as to radically expand the power of the executive branch relative to the legislative branch, we have not just a democratic or constitutional problem but a rule of law one too. A government writing its own rules for how to govern is not exactly what the latter has in mind.

What, therefore, are the nature of complaints made when executive lawmaking is scrutinised through a rule of law lens? The experience of the Covid-19 pandemic is instructive here, in so far as it brought with it a preponderance of rule of law-based complaints in response to the scale of executive lawmaking there seen. These complaints carried a range of messages. Some were concerned about the concentration of executive power and the corresponding retreat of the legislature (Webber, 2020), demonstrating the crossover between our brief study of emergencies and worries about executive lawmaking per se. Other complaints were raised against the formal characteristics of the latter (Carmichael & Webber, 2021), as measured against one or other account of the principles we examined in Section 1.3.2. Still further objections took aim at the prolific use of public health advice that sent strong messages about obligation, and yet lacked the legal pedigree necessary to render such obligations enforceable (Hickman, 2020).[57]

---

[57] We return to the phenomenon of soft law in Section 3.2.3.

We expand our consideration of the form(s) of law in rule of law thought in Section 3.2. For present purposes however it is worth noticing the increasing interest among scholars towards forms of executive lawmaking that carry the superficial trappings of law, but which function in practice to expand rather than to constrain executive power (Cohn, 2021). Inquiry of this kind shares some of its concerns with studies of 'abusive constitutionalism' (section titled Emergencies), but its more granular focus deserves emphasis in its own right. Though not new – Lon Fuller's analysis (1958: 648–61) of the legal forms and practices of the Nazi order was an undertaking of this kind – the constitutional context of such inquiries does much to enrich the scope of rule of law thought in its connection to the habits of contemporary constitutional practice.

Finally, a word about terminology. Grievances about the conduct of actors of the executive branch are often cast in the language of 'accountability'. Certainly, accountability and the rule of law are close cousins when the demand at issue is that political power be answerable to law. But in the context of a constitutional order, calls for accountability can also attach to a range of wider political conventions and practices. The (theoretical) expectation in the Westminster parliamentary tradition that a responsible minister of government will resign for failures committed on their watch is an example. Highlighting the wider domain within which the idea of accountability can reside, as compared to the rule of law, might seem to some like an exercise of splitting hairs. Yet several of the worries just examined were not squarely or solely worries about accountability. They were worries about the fate of *law*, specifically, as a constraint on political power.

2.6 Controversies

Its historical tilt towards the protection of individual rights, especially rights to property, from the encroachments of an interventionist state is the primary ideological entanglement with which the rule of law has been associated (Section 2.4.2). Influenced especially by the work of Friedrich Hayek, on this conception the idea of the rule of law is inseparable from a cluster of social, political, and institutional commitments that together reflect the view that to be a free individual is to be free from the coercive powers of government specifically (Section 1.5.2). According to this logic, a society that engages in economic planning is by definition *not* one governed by the rule of law (Hayek, 2007: 119).

Arguments as polemical as this kind rarely escape pushback. Initially at least, the reply to Hayek articulated an opposing dogmatism. If the rule of law is and does what Hayek says it is and does, the argument ran, then it is by definition the enemy of the welfare state: a political order that supports democratically mandated government action to redistribute private wealth for social and collective causes.[58] This reply became known as the 'equality critique' of the rule of law. On this view, the negative conception of liberty (freedom from the encroachments of government power) that animates orthodox rule of law thought is fundamentally at odds with a political order that assigns a role to (legislated) law to foster socioeconomic conditions aimed at promoting the equality and agency of all persons.

The rejection of the idea of the rule of law by supporters of the welfare state is an important moment in its modern history (Loughlin, 2018: 660–1). The equality critique called attention to the apparent oppositions between liberty and equality, or negative and positive liberty, that were assumed to travel with the ideas of the rule of law and the welfare state respectively. Not all, however, were convinced that these oppositions were necessarily so stark. A more constructive conversation thus emerged, concerned with how far these oppositions should be taken (Hutchinson & Monahan, 1987; Hutchinson, 1999) and what might be lost through overstating them. For scholars like Bill Scheuerman, for example, '*both* the rule of law *and* a reconstructed, more emancipatory welfare state' are possible, and necessitate scepticism towards those 'who insist we must choose one or the other but cannot have both' (Scheuerman, 1994: 195).

This controversy is important because it asks us to reflect on whether the idea of the rule of law is irretrievably tethered to one particular vision of politics. A well-known sub-controversy within this space was the conclusion of the late twentieth century Marxist historian, E. P. Thompson (1977: 267), that the rule of law is 'an unqualified human good'. Thompson's commitment to interpreting legal, social, and economic arrangements through a Marxist lens would ordinarily have supported the conclusion that the rule of law is a mere instrument used by elites to sustain a political and economic order suited to their interests, and against those of the working classes. Although his famous study of a 1723 English statute that prohibited shooting of deer by peasants provided abundant evidence of the latter, to Thompson's surprise it also revealed something else: the law *sometimes* protected the peasants.

Thompson's unexpectedly pro-rule of law conclusion was more nuanced than is often portrayed. It spoke above all to the procedural regularities involved in the application of the law by courts to individual cases (Hay, 2021). Still, it was met with the response that these apparent procedural goods are no more than an ideological mask (Horwitz, 1977), justifying the rule of law's lack of concern for questions of substantive justice (Sypnowich, 1999: 183).[59] Such is the

---

[58] Hence Shklar's astute observation (1987: 29) that the 'negative mirror image of the Dicey–Hayek model of the Rule of Law can be found among the radical legal critics of liberalism'.

[59] See also the critical interrogation of the association between the rule of law is the rule of rules in Radin (1989) and Hutchinson (1999). See further Section 3.2.1.

business of argument. But for those interested to explore the possibility of a middle ground, the task is to reflect on *which* aspects of the rule of law are thought to be incompatible with redistributive political causes, and which aspects are considered to have more promise in this regard (Scheuerman, 1994: 200).

More recent engagements with the ideological baggage that travels with the rule of law can be seen to tread this somewhat quieter political path. Key questions here include how the idea might productively be reconciled with the positive work of public law in the context of a well-functioning administrative state.[60] Engagements that seek a 'normatively robust conception of the rule of law that does not minimise or deprecate the mission of public administration' (Waldron, 2015: 57) are obviously still political, in the sense that they are well aware of the historical tilt of the rule of law towards a politics of small government, the protection of property and contract, the centrality of the market mechanism, or some combination thereof.[61] But these engagements insist on working *with* the idea, rather than against it, to investigate how it might support more participatory and inclusive political agendas (Barber, 2018: 100–4). Waldron's contention (2012b) that the rule of law should endorse and applaud the use of legislation to achieve valid social objectives is one example, and Raz's argument (2019: 14) that 'the virtue of the rule of law lies in tending to secure that the government acts with the manifest intention of serving the interests of the governed' might be regarded as another.

2.6.1 The Ideology of Rule of Law Discourse

The rhetorical heft of the rule of law is a force in its own right, carrying 'powerful overtones of positive evaluation' (Waldron, 2021: 128; compare Seppänen, 2016). This is why it is important to reflect on what work the apparently good reputation of the rule of law is doing within a given engagement with the idea.[62] This question is especially salient in relation to the phenomenon of 'rule of law discourse' with which we became acquainted in Section 2.3.2.

It is critical to appreciate the temporal context of rule of law discourse as a late twentieth and early twenty-first century phenomenon, and its association with neoliberalism specifically. As explained in Section 1.5.2, neoliberalism

---

[60] This is an attempt to push against the primary historical narrative in which the rule of law is overly associated with the work of judicial review of administrative action (section titled 'Constraining the Executive') in ensuring that government power does not encroach upon the individual, except as prescribed by law.

[61] Jeremy Waldron (2021) especially emphasises the influence of the thought of John Locke in this regard.

[62] For an historical analysis of how the rule of law functioned discursively to do particular kinds of justificatory work to support the cause of the British Empire, see Lino (2018).

refers to a political philosophy that conceives of the role of government primarily in terms of facilitating conditions in which the market can take root as the central organising mechanism of social and political order. It takes little to recognise Hayek as the father of neoliberalism so understood, and of the particular vision of the rule of law promoted within it. Relevantly for present purposes, the key historical shift to understand is that, alongside the growth of international law and international institutions, the second half of the twentieth century saw dramatic institutional shifts from 'welfare state' to 'neoliberal' models of government across the world. These political and institutional shifts were however not only facilitated by governments of the wealthy nations of the west. Their replication and transplantation also became the mission of international rule of law promotion and measurement initiatives.[63]

The ever-consolidating association between the rule of law and the neoliberal political agenda within this global practice is now impossible to miss (Tamanaha, 2008). So too is the role of rule of law discourse as its vehicle. As Humphreys (2021: 477) has explained, in this era rule of law discourse has become an *economic* discourse used to refer primarily 'to a set of measures aiming to reduce the role of government in economic life and sharpen the boundary between public and private interests'. Initially directed at the independence of judiciaries to ensure secure enforcement of property and contractual rights, as it expanded rule of law discourse 'enhanced the privatization of state enterprises and protections of investors' rights' (Humphreys, 2021: 477–8).

Bringing these details into the picture is important not merely to witness the ideological tilt of rule of law discourse as a distinctive late twentieth and early twenty-first century phenomenon, but also to assess the fate of companion ideas within it. It is common, for example, to see the rule of law paired with democracy in such discourse. Yet as Joel Ngugi (2005) has analysed, this discursive pairing masks how the practical operationalisation of the neoliberal conception that informs the rule of law side of that companionship effectively forecloses the kind of participatory politics advertised in the democracy side. According to Ngugi (2005: 516), rule of law promotion projects 'predetermine politics', insulating a particular neoliberal vision of the good 'from the reach of political debate, consensus or revision by the participants in a given polity' while embedding the formal institutional trappings of the rule of law. Analyses of this kind make clear that to engage critically with rule of law discourse, it is essential to pay attention to what actually happens on the ground, behind, beneath or alongside its rhetoric (Chalmers & Pahuja, 2021; Humphreys, 2021).

---

[63] See especially footnotes 19 and 20.

What happens next? The argument might be put that the pendulum has swung too far towards a neoliberal conception of the rule of law and its associated values – at least in global rule of law practice – such that it is no longer possible to recruit the term without bringing a particular set of ideological attachments along for the ride. Perhaps Judith Shklar was right when she suggested 'it would not be difficult to show that the phrase "the Rule of Law" has become meaningless thanks to ideological abuse and general over-use' (Shklar, 1987: 1). Be that as it may or may not, the idea of the rule of law has had many adventures in its life so far, and each has been associated different visions of politics (Loughlin, 2018). This is something that we should simply expect from an idea that has always straddled political and legal thought and practice, and always will.

3 Revisiting the Rule of Law

3.1 Why Revisit?

The stated intention of this Element to *revisit* the rule of law is in keeping with its era and with the idea itself.[64] The recent explosion of perspective-seeking works on the rule of law is one way through which this revisitation has been pursued (Waldron, 2016; Meierhenrich & Loughlin, 2021), while individual theorists returning to update past work is another (Raz, 2019). Both enterprises reflect what we can anticipate from the life of an 'essentially contested concept'. Its meaning, features, implications, and applications are inherently revisable in light of changing practices of law and governance, or shifts in our thinking about them.

This final part pursues a different kind of revisitation. Its motivating thought is that to revisit the rule of law needs also to be an exercise in noticing what remains under-examined or underdeveloped within theoretical treatment of the idea, and asking why. A number of inquiries could have occupied the focus of this exercise.[65] Our focus however will be on two domains of inquiry that remain surprisingly underdeveloped in scholarship on the rule of law. The first concerns the assumptions about the form(s) of law that shape – and arguably limit – theoretical engagement with the idea. The second concerns the people of the rule of law: who's in, who's out, who is overlooked, and why. Together these two inquiries bring us full circle to the emphasis given at the outset to the rule of law's core political demand that ruler and ruled alike must be subordinate to law. Our objective now is to dig more deeply into this demand, and to reflect on the new frontiers of rule of law thought that might open up through doing so.

3.2 Legal Form in Rule of Law Thought

Talk of 'form' usually enters rule of law thought in association with 'formal' conceptions of the idea that make demands on the form that legal norms should take in an order committed to the rule of law (Section 1.3.1; Gardner, 2012). The idea of form with which we engage in this section is more

---

[64] Martin Loughlin (2018) has nicely captured the modern history of the idea of the rule of law as a progression marked by stages of inventing, rejecting, shifting, reviving, recrafting, relocating, and reifying, culminating in its present apotheosis.

[65] Leading examples include the ever-widening body of theoretically inflected scholarship that seeks to extend rule of law thought beyond its traditional focus on governmental arrangements internal to the state, such as the extension of rule of law demands to private actors (West, 2011; Ramirez, 2013; Sempill, 2017); the application of rule of law thought to the international sphere (Crawford, 2003; Chesterman, 2008; Beaulac, 2009; Nijman, 2015); and the provocation to rule of law thought from legal pluralism (Tamanaha, 2011; Grenfell, 2013; Lefkowitz, 2020).

complex. It speaks to the shape of legal arrangements associated – or not – with the rule of law. We begin with the dominant assumption that the rule of law is the rule of generally applicable rules, before revisiting the legal form long maligned as the enemy of the rule of law: discretion. From there we are well positioned to ask whether new governmental forms are friends or foes of the rule of law.

3.2.1 The Rule of Rules?

The requirement that law consists of general rules is often considered the essence of the rule of law (Raz, 1979: 215). In some respects, this is justified: few would dispute that rules are the archetypal legal form. The idea that law in a rule of law order has general application is also critical to how the latter is thought to foster the equality of all before the law. Here, again, its association with rules makes sense.

Rules, however, are not the only legal form in the rule of law's toolbox. When philosophers seek to highlight this, they often do so by noticing that law is also comprised of standards and principles (Waldron, 2016: 8.2). What this expansion of the categories of legal artefacts that comprise the law of the rule of law means depends on the theory in play. For example, if one subscribes to the view that the rule of law consists in the predictable application of rules, the more open formulation of standards and principles will likely provoke controversy (Waldron, 2021: 124–5). Yet as we learned throughout Part 2, the basis of objections in the name of the rule of law to different *kinds* of law often lies in ideological commitments that regard virtually all powers of government as coercive, and which tolerate only the strictest negative (freedom from) conceptions of the rule of law.

Other complexities have developed around the rule of law's presumptive attachment to general rules. These are especially reflected in theories of regulation, which often position the looser, formally diverse, and more horizontal modes of regulatory law in opposition to an idea of law as a framework of rules (Westerman, 2018: 141–67). These assumptions about what law in the context of regulation is *not* have often led theorists of regulation to distance that endeavour from the ideal of the rule of law. Yet here again certain theoretical assumptions and manoeuvres are in play. Theories of regulatory law that sideline the relevance of the rule of law ideal tend to attach to theories of the rule of law capable of supporting such a move (McDonald, 2004).

These tensions might however invite revisitation in circumstances in which their implications have not yet been fully tested. Insisting that regulatory law is entirely different to 'traditional' law, or labelling all modes of law as 'regulatory', can carry consequences for 'ordinary people's understandings of what the state is, does, and ought to do' (Arthurs, 2005: 830): precisely the kinds of understandings that have long preoccupied rule of law thought. Sidelining the idea of the rule of law might also be misplaced in situations where subjects wish to make much stronger demands on political power than is possible within the more horizontal and less coercive arrangements associated with regulation. Environmental protection is an example.

Much may accordingly be at stake in an insufficiently interrogated confla- tion of the rule of law with the rule of rules if such operates to set directions of thought that move away from its core political demand of mutual subor- dination to law. As is always the case, much will depend on how the rule of law is theorised in relation to these questions. But as we will see next and develop further in Section 3.4.2, much will also depend on a heightened awareness of the non-neutrality of different legal forms in terms of how they position the rule of law's people, in relation to each other as well as in relation to the law that rules.

3.2.2 Revisiting Discretion

Discretion has long provoked panic in the hearts of rule of law theorists, who at their most fearful have regarded it as little more than arbitrary power in legal clothing. Certainly, in terms of its form, discretion is entirely different to rules. Discretion leaves its repository 'free to make a choice between possible courses of action or inaction' (Davis, 1969: 4). This crucial feature of freedom of choice on the part of the repository, whatever its degree, necessarily produces a different form of legal relation to that which arises within an order of rules.

The preoccupation of rule of law thought with general rules can distract us from the political or power dimensions of 'law' in the phrase 'the rule of law'. Like enacted rules and the rulings of courts, the legal pedigree (section titled The Executive as Lawmaker) of discretionary powers is usually not in question. Most are expressly granted to a particular office holder by statute. This mark of legal pedigree does not however change the fact that discretionary powers are powers in a way that rules are not. They give their repository choices as to possible courses of action in relation to the circumstances of the person subject to them.

In rule of law theory, the idea that discretion is little more than arbitrary power in legal clothing is most strongly associated with the thought of A. V. Dicey (Section 1.5.1), though it is notable that his complaints did not extend to the many judicial discretions that are part of the common law method that he and Hayek after him (Sections 1.5.2 and 2.5.2) so revered. This is perhaps because discretion in the judicial context is treated more as a question about law than about the rule of law (Sandro, 2022: 116–68). The kind of discretion targeted by Dicey was administrative: that reposed in actors of the executive (Section 2.5.3). We have seen that Dicey, in a similar vein to Hayek after him, bemoaned legislatively mandated encroachments on private law rights associated with arrival of the 'welfare state' (Sections 2.5.2 and 2.6). His angst towards discretion, therefore, was not simply about arbitrary power per se. It was tethered to his defence of England's existing political and institutional order.

It was impatience with the extent to which the ghost of Dicey hovered over Anglo-American legal thought that led Kenneth Culp Davis (1969) to undertake his seminal work on 'discretionary justice'. Davis's complaint was that extravagant theories of the rule of law which assumed that enacted rules were the only legal form (and courts the only supervisory institutions) through which the rule of law could be maintained had discouraged scholars from engaging seriously with discretion as a site of legal inquiry (Davis, 1969: 30, 28–41). Davis did not doubt that discretion could be of questionable legality. His point was that not *all* discretion is necessarily at odds with the rule of law, or indeed with just decisions in individual cases. If appropriately confined and structured, the exercise of discretionary powers could be compatible with the rule of law (Davis, 1969: 4, 30).

The main rule of law question in relation to discretion is thus thought to concern what degree of curtailment of discretionary powers is ideal in order to for such powers to be compliant with the rule of law (Raz, 2019: 4). This states the key problem, but we might here push it further. As scholars of discretion have taught us, discretionary administrative power can have both 'individualised' aspects which attend to the particular attributes and circumstances of the individual subject to it, as well as 'policy-based' aspects that allow room for politics and political judgement (Galligan, 1996). To better appreciate how and why discretion presents a dilemma for the rule of law, therefore, we need to bring the latter's core political demand of mutual subordination to law back into view. Leading with this demand, we see that the most serious rule of law worry presented by discretionary powers consists in the space taken up by political considerations within them – and the options available, if any, to the subject of such a power to do anything about it (Cartier, 2009; Rundle, 2021a).

3.2.3 Friends or Foes of the Rule of Law?

The structure, operation and content of what is often called the 'administrative state' has been held out as evidence that law in practice does not always look the way it does in theory (Rubin, 1989). As we have already encountered in our brief engagement with the fluid and horizontal forms regulatory law (Section 3.2.1), contemporary government action is channelled through a far greater proliferation of legal forms and technologies than those which have traditionally preoccupied rule of law thought. How, therefore, might we revisit the rule of law in relation to these developments?

We might begin by recognising that even if such developments seem new, the rule of law questions raised by them will often be enduring. The phenomenon of soft law provides an illustration (Creyke & McMillan, 2008). Whether used as a tool to aid consistency in administrative decision-making, or issued as guidance to subjects about the operation of 'hard' law, soft law often looks like law and often also does law's normative work in guiding conduct, but lacks legal pedigree (section titled The Executive as Lawmaker). Soft law accordingly raises a range of rule of law questions. On the one hand it might be lauded for how it aids decision-makers to make consistent decisions across like cases, or for how it helps subjects to understand what the law asks of them (Crawford, 2020). On the other, there are concerns about the overuse of soft law in circumstances where democratically legitimated hard law is meant to rule (section titled The Executive as Lawmaker).

The now ubiquitous practice of contracted-out government service delivery (or outsourcing) has been much less interrogated in rule of law terms. Recalling that the protection of private law rights in contract has long been regarded as among its core offerings, we might say that the rule of law does important work in providing security to the parties to an outsourcing contract. But what about those subject to government functions performed this way? Such persons have no apparent place within a rule of law story concerned principally with the enforcement of contract because ordinarily they possess no contractual rights. We could also ask whether facilitating the performance by private contractors of government functions authorised and delineated through legislation might change the law in the rule of law, in so far that such functions must be translated into services or tasks capable of forming the subject matter of contract. Here we might wonder where translation ends and transformation begins.

It is the rise of algorithmic decision-making, however, that has generated the most attention among those concerned to illuminate the relationship between the rule of law and new forms of government action. Many of the worries here, such as who is answerable for the work of these technologies and how, are familiar (Carney, 2019; Zalnieriute et al., 2019). Concerns are also regularly voiced about the lack of transparency and potential arbitrariness of automated technologies, including how they prevent subjects from knowing how the law is being applied to them (Hildebrandt, 2016; Kennedy, 2020; Ng, 2021; Maxwell & Tomlinson, 2022). While the potential for such technologies to produce results that are consistent or predictable is lauded by some (Zalnieriute et al., 2019), the potential loss of contestation in relation to the application of law worries others (Hildebrandt, 2018).

These objections and endorsements call upon familiar ideas in the history of rule of law thought. Yet computer-assisted technologies arguably also introduce entirely new puzzles into the picture. Recommendations that there should always be a 'human in the loop', for example, express concern that the pendulum has swung too far such that the human being and distinctly human cognitive and moral capacities need to be pushed to the foreground of discussion about the implications of such technologies for the rule of law (Jones, 2017; Bateman, 2020; Pasquale, 2020). Though a perhaps unexpected catalyst for a fundamental question, the advent of algorithmic decision-making invites us to reflect on how and in what ways the rule of law fundamentally depends on its people, in terms of who they are expected to be as well as how they are expected to act.

3.3 The People of the Rule of Law

The rule of law would be nothing without the agency of the people who carry its burdens and benefit from its contributions. Be that as it may, theories of the rule of law tend to implicate ideas about its people more often than they expressly articulate those ideas. For example, if the rule of law is understood as a condition of government directed at preventing the possibility of arbitrary power, then presumably it aims to do so for the benefit of those subject to such rule: the rule of law's subjects thus appear by implication. The same goes for the rule of law's officials. If the rule of law prescribes that political power must be held and exercised in a particular way, then those prescriptions must attach to someone: its officials.

The purpose of the remainder of this Element is to think more deeply about the people of the rule of law than may have been customary in theoretical treatment of the idea to this point: who they are, the relationships between them, and why it has persistently been the case that certain people are missing within – or missing out from – rule of law thought and practice alike.

3.3.1 Subjects

To the extent that they figure at all, subjects within rule of law theory are typically cast as individuals doing or possessing particular things, like having an interest in their individual liberty, or being the holder of particular rights in private or public law. Sometimes these subjects take on more distinct identities, such as all (natural and artificial) persons within a territory, or the subjects of a particular nation state. At their least defined the subjects of the rule of law emerge as little more than undifferentiated units of a society or population.

We might begin an attempt to excavate the subject from rule of law thought with the safe assumption that subjectivity in rule of law thought will be shaped by the particular conception of the rule of law in play. For example, in those 'substantive' conceptions of the rule of law that rank respect for human rights among its requirements (Section 1.3.1), the subject of the rule of law will be presumed to be the bearer of human rights in addition to whatever other characteristics they might possess. The conception of law in play will also matter. If the 'law' in the rule of law is presumed to take the form of rules, for example, its subject will be expected to possess the rational and moral capacities necessary to follow such rules and to be answerable for their breach.

We can also readily assume that subjectivity in rule of law thought will be shaped by claims made about its purposes, contributions, or values (Section 2.2.1). For example, if the claim is that observance of the principles of the rule of law fosters a particular experience of liberty, or the recognition of human dignity, or the capacity to enforce legal rights in contract or property, a particular conception of the subject will be needed to lend support to such claims. We might equally see shifts in how subjectivity is understood depending on whether it is presented in singular or plural form. The subject might appear in singular form, for example, when the analysis at issue concerns the significance of particular legal procedures, like the right to be heard in relation to an allegation (Section 2.5.2). By contrast, the rule of law's subjects might be more likely to appear in plural form when its political dimensions are in focus, such as in the idea that subjects of the rule of law are those who are free from the encroachments of government other than through that which is prescribed by law.

These observations are helpful, and likely uncontroversial. But might it possible to say something more precise about how subjectivity within the rule of law can be theorised? The provocation developed here is that we can indeed go further in theorising the subject of the rule of law if we remind ourselves that the rule of law is an idea that straddles political and legal thought. Following this logic, subjectivity to and within the rule of law must have both political and legal dimensions. We begin with the former.

Subjectivity: The Political Dimension

Throughout this Element we have emphasised that the core political demand of the rule of law is the idea of mutual subordination to law. Those in possession of political power must not only govern through law, but be answerable to its demands in the same way that subjects are answerable to those demands. As we learned in Section 1.2.3, the political demand of mutual subordination to law is crucial to the claimed difference between the rule of law and rule by law.

The implications of this demand for the rule of law's subjects are profound. To recall earlier discussions, if arranging political power this way offers such 'goods' to its subjects as liberty (Section 2.2.3) and dignity (Section 2.4.2), these are inseparable from whether those in possession of political power act in accordance with what is required of them by law. We return to this figure of the legally constrained official momentarily. We need first to trace out the legal dimension of subjectivity to and within the rule of law, and its relation to the political dimension.

Subjectivity: The Legal Dimension

If the rule of law is the rule of *law*, then it seems logical to begin exploring the legal dimensions of subjectivity to and within the rule of law through the idea of legal personhood. Here we will take our lead from Ngaire Naffine's (2003) analysis of the three conceptions of the legal person that recur in legal discourse: Person 1 (P1), Person 2 (P2), and Person 3 (P3) respectively.[66]

P1 is a purely legal conception of legal personhood that derives from the idea of legal rights: an abstract being who has capacity to bear legal rights, and whose existence depends on the existence of law. This is the conception of legal personhood compatible with theories of legal rights as well as with the idea that non-human entities such as corporations are legal persons.

In stark contrast to P1, P2 is unapologetically human: the product of the thought of those who suggest that legal rights are 'natural' to human beings, or who regard the human being as the basis of legal personality. P2 is thus readily recognisable as the conception of legal personhood underscoring legalised human rights. Like P1, P2 is a person to whom law and legal relationships might attach, but unlike P1, P2 relies on their humanness rather than law for their existence (Naffine, 2003: 358).

It is P3, however, who Naffine suggests has had the most pervasive influence on legal thought. P3 is 'the ideal (if not the actual) legal actor' whose defining feature is their rationality. The quintessential responsible agent, equipped with rational capacity not only for making choices but also for taking (legal) responsibility for actions attaching to those choices, P3 can clearly be recognised as the person of contract and criminal law, as well as the conception of legal personhood informing ideas about legal competence, capacity, and guardianship

---

[66] Relevantly to our discussion in Section 3.4.1, Naffine's body of work on legal personhood is an outgrowth of her work in feminist legal theory concerned with which, if any, conception of legal personhood might support the normative aims of feminist legal thought. Naffine ultimately chooses P1 as the most promising conception of legal personhood from the point of view of feminist legal theory precisely for its moral, social, and biological featurelessness.

(Naffine, 2003: 362, 364). It follows that not all human persons can be a legal person in the P3 sense.

If the rule of law is understood primarily as the rule of rules, then P3 lies at the heart of rule of law orthodoxy as much as they do legal thought more generally. But is this enough to theorise the subject of the rule of law, specifically? In particular, might we need to think more deeply about in what subjectivity under the rule of law consists if we are to determine whether it might require something more, from its subjects, than simply being a receptacle of rights (P1), a human being (P2), or having the capacity to contract or to follow rules (P3)?

Again we might benefit from returning to the claimed distinction between the rule of law and rule by law. When law is understood in terms of a model of rules, the legal person is presupposed to have the capacity to follow rules and to be answerable for their breach: P3. The problem, however, is that this conception of legal personhood seems to fit as well with the idea of rule by law as it does with the idea of the rule of law. This suggests that if the latter is meant to be distinguishable from the former on the basis that it offers something more to its subjects, then it follows that something more than the classic P3 conception of the responsible rule-governed agent is needed to give content to subjectivity to and within the rule of law.

We can develop this thought further by returning to the phenomenon of discretion (Section 3.2.2). While theories of the rule of law have long been preoccupied with this troublesome legal form, theories of legal personhood appear to have neglected it. This is telling us something important. It suggests that a theory of subjectivity to and within the rule of law cannot be supplied solely by conceptions of legal personhood. Rather, any such theory must *also* incorporate the political dimensions of the rule of law.

The idea proposed here is that subjectivity to and within the rule of law needs to be understood in association with the particular species of agency – *legal* agency – that such a condition is thought to foster in its subjects (Rundle, 2019: 24). We can arrive at what is distinctive about legal agency by asking what the rule of law's core political demand of mutual subordination to law requires of its people. Most obviously, the idea of mutual subordination carries inferences of constraint and restraint. The thought is that all agents in the political order, officials and subjects alike, are constrained by the demands of the law and will restrain their own actions to ensure that those constraints are observed. But there is clearly more to the rule of law than constraint and restraint. As an ideal – a normative goal – in the rule of law officials and subjects alike must also direct their agency towards the achievement of its aspirations. Crucially, for subjects expressing that agency will sometimes translate into a demand on officials that they, too, comply with the (rule of) law.[67]

Subjectivity within a political order committed to the rule of law must therefore be comprised not only of legal personhood, but also of the capacity on the part of the subject to make a law-based demand on the rule of law's officials in accordance with the political demand of mutual subordination to law. We will see shortly how those who are missing or missing out from the rule of law are explicitly or implicitly refused the benefits of this demand (Section 3.4.1). But first we must meet the person whose conduct is crucial to whether those benefits accrue at all.

3.3.2 Officials

A number of personae spring to mind when we speak of the officials of the rule of law. The first is that of the legislator: the maker of the enacted general rules around which so much of legal thought is built. In theoretical engagements with the rule of law, this official might appear in a number of different forms, from the law-giving ruler (Fuller, 1969: 33) to the sovereign lawmaker (Hobbes, 2017) to the de-personified institution of the parliament.

The most encountered official within theories of the rule of law, however, is the judge. Whether in personified form or represented in the institution of a court, theories of and theoretical engagements with the rule of law see this figure interpreting and applying statutes, developing the common law, enforcing legal rights in contract or property, adjudicating disputes impartially, conducting judicial review of government action, applying the procedures of criminal law, and more. Each of these activities is associated not just with the work of judges or courts generally, but also with the work of the rule of law specifically.

As is also the case for its subjects, the ways in which the officials of the rule of law might appear will depend on how the latter is theorised. For example, the idea of the official implicated in a 'formal' conception of the rule of law (Section 1.3.2) would be someone who complies with the rule of law's prescriptions irrespective of the justice or injustice of the content of laws so made. By contrast, if the focus is on the rule of law's role in protecting private property rights (Section 1.5.2), the official might present as a person of conservative political comportment committed to maintaining the socioeconomic status quo through the careful incremental development of private law protections. Differently again, those who prioritise inquiry into the 'teleology' or purpose

---

[67] For example, judicial review in administrative law involves the subject of an administrative decision seeking a remedy from a court to direct an administrative official to comply with the law.

of the rule of law (Section 1.4) might conceive of its official as someone poised to 'temper' power through the enforcement of context-specific legal constraints appropriate to particular sociological conditions.

The point being made is not just that particular theoretical approaches to the rule of law will implicate different conceptions of its officials, but that the *comportment* of those officials is critical to the conception of the rule of law in play. The tendency for rule of law theory to emphasise capacities for reason and impartiality, for example, shows just how influential the figure of the judge has been to our thinking around the idea. Indeed, according to Judith Shklar (1987: 1, 3), in its emphasis on the rule of reason the Aristotelian tradition of rule of law thought positions 'the character one must impute to those who make legal judgments' at the centre of the idea itself, demanding that its official is a person who possesses a 'constant disposition to act fairly and lawfully'.

The extent to which rule of law thought continues to be dominated by the judge as its paragon official likely has much to do with the dominance of legal theorists in developing contemporary theories of the rule of law. We have learned a lot about how judges relate to the law and the rule of law alike through this work in legal theory.[68] But as we saw earlier (Section 3.2.3), 'official' action in modern governmental conditions takes a wide variety of forms, such that identifying *who* are the rule of law's officials presents both conceptual and practical puzzles.[69] Who, for example, are the officials of the rule of law within an instance of contracted-out government service delivery? Or in a system of automated government decision-making?[70] Jeremy Waldron (2016: 3.4) makes an important point when he observes that although the rule of law generates a presumption in favour of the liberty of subjects, a contrary presumption applies to its officials: we want these people only to act 'under express legal authorization'. Thus, even if we were to designate the persons (and machines!) of new governmental forms as officials of the rule of law, there are still questions to answer about how to pull them into its demands.

Underlying such questions is a challenge as old as the idea of the rule of law itself. When the ground underneath it shifts, we will sometimes need not merely to reappraise the demands carried by the idea, but also the people we associate with those demands. In a far greater sense than seen in relation to its subjects,

---

[68] Comparably less emphasis has been given to how the rule of law's officials comport themselves in relation to the rule of law's subjects: an important exception is work that emphasises how the procedural dimensions of the rule of law foster respect the dignity of the subject (Section 2.5.1; see further Section 3.4).

[69] See further Section 2.5.3.

[70] This question becomes more complex still when automated systems perform the work of lawyers: see Gowder (2018) and Hildebrandt (2018) for reflections on this point.

theories of the rule of law must be supple enough to accommodate the sheer variety of people, roles and institutions associated with those who wield power within a political order ostensibly committed to the ideal. This is a significant demand on rule of law thought in its own right. But it is made more significant still when we bring (back) in the people at the receiving end of political power held and exercised this way.

3.4 Thinking Relationally about the Rule of Law

If much of what is going on in the rule of law boils down to how the officials of the political order act towards its subjects, then the quality of relationship that holds between the people of the rule of law goes to the very heart of the idea. Moreover, as the 'of' in the phrase 'the rule of law' signals, the relationship of both to the law is equally crucial.

Different ways of thinking about the rule of law implicate different ways of describing the character of both kinds of relationship. For those who approach the rule of law through the particular substantive and methodological commitments of analytic philosophy (Section 1.3), the 'basic intuition' from which the idea of the rule of law derives is that the law must be capable of guiding the behaviour of its subjects (Raz, 1979: 214). On this view, the relationship between the rule of law's people can be described primarily in terms of the imperative of guidance. Whether seeing the relationship this way prioritises the interests of the rule of law's officials more than it does its subjects is a question on which minds may differ.

What is clear, however, is that other ways of thinking about the rule of law present a richer relational picture. Earlier we learned that the rule of law is associated with the legitimacy of political rule, primarily because it is thought to be a mode of political rule that fosters individual liberty (Section 2.2.3). Again, this can to some extent cut both ways: the officials of a rule of law order have much to gain if its subjects regard their authority as legitimate as this undoubtedly aids the cause of their rule. But as we emphasised in Section 2.2.3, legitimacy is of its nature something conferred. The primary perspective that matters to whether political rule is regarded as legitimate will always be the perspective of the subject.

Pushing this perspective forward was one of the aims of the mid-twentieth century legal philosopher, Lon Fuller. We were briefly introduced to Fuller's thought in association with the eight principles thought to comprise his 'account' of the rule of law in Section 1.3.2, and again in the context of our examination of arguments about the conceptual separability of law and the rule of law in Section 1.6. Fuller however never set out to produce an account of the rule of law per se.[71] Indeed, he expressly eschewed the analytic philosopher's preoccupation with concepts, preferring instead to view both law and the rule of law as practices dependent on human effort whose existence could only ever be a matter of degree (Fuller, 1969).

Recent scholarship on Fuller has sought to shift understandings of his contribution to rule of law theory towards the quality of relationships that he thought must obtain within a commitment to the rule of law (Rundle, 2019, 2021b). As Fuller saw things, maintaining such a condition required a 'cooperative effort' between legal officials and legal subjects (Fuller, 1969: 216), as well as 'fidelity to law' on the part of both (Fuller, 1958). The reason why Fuller was so preoccupied with these relationships is because he wanted to emphasise the conditions necessary for law to be *authoritative* for those subject to it. Fuller thought that a relationship in which the official merely acted upon the subject was not a relationship that could plausibly sustain the conditions necessary for the subject's acceptance of that official's authority (Fuller, 1969: 163). He insisted that something closer to 'reciprocity', rendered concrete through the operation of the principles we associate with the rule of law, is needed if the subject is to have a basis for accepting the law's authority or that of any official action taken in accordance with it (Fuller, 1969: 39–40).

Returning to the claimed distinction between the rule of law and rule by law helps to illuminate the argument Fuller was trying to make. As explained in Section 1.2.3, rule by law and the rule of law can look a lot alike from the perspective of those with the power to rule: the officials. The same, however, does not hold at the other end of the relationship. The rule of law significantly alters the position of the person on the bottom as compared to how they would be positioned in an order of rule by law. Because of its core political demand of mutual subordination to law, in the rule of law the subject should be able to make a law-based demand on political power that they would not be able to make in a political order of rule by law. Viewed through a relational lens, therefore, we can see that the key difference between rule by law and the rule of law boils down to the different position occupied by the subject within each.

The question for our purposes is whether giving greater attention to these relational dimensions of the rule of law might generate a productive shift in how we think about the idea generally. In our discussion of the enduring concern of rule of law thought with arbitrary power (Section 1.2.2), we noted that it is important to be aware of the direction of thought in which a particular preoccupation of rule of law theory might take us. When we say that a particular instance of practice is contrary to the rule of law because it amounts to an

---

[71] Fuller actually used the term 'the rule of law' very rarely in his writings, but notably did so in relation to his eighth principle of congruence between official action and declared rule: 'if the rule of law does not mean this, it means nothing' (Fuller, 1969: 210).

arbitrary exercise of power, the message we are usually trying to convey is that what is occurring is something that the rule of law is meant to prevent or protect against. We make that point by focusing on the particular *thing* that captures the worry at hand: arbitrary power.

The provocation advanced here is that we might do better to engage more directly with the relationship that is implicit in this most enduring complaint of rule of law thought. What is *always* askew in circumstances that give rise to the potential for arbitrary power is the structure of the relationship between the official and the subject. When the official is positioned to wield excessive or insufficiently bounded power over the subject, the law is not disciplining the agency of official and subject in anywhere near the same way. The complaint, in essence, is that the rule of law's core political demand of mutual subordination to law has been knocked off balance.

Commencing inquiry from the starting point of the relationships that should hold between the rule of law's people accommodates rather than sidelines the tradition's longstanding preoccupation with arbitrary power. But what a relational emphasis achieves that is not achieved by attention to arbitrariness alone is to bring the rule of law's core political demand of mutual subordination to law into the foreground. Instead of focusing on the thing that is meant to capture the worry at hand – arbitrary power – we focus instead on what is going on between the rule of law's people in relation to that core political demand. From this position we are better placed to answer more specific questions such as *why* mutual subordination to law is faring so badly in a given instance.

Taking rule of law thought more consciously in this direction also helps to tie together a number of points made in our discussion so far, and to lay the foundations for the remainder to come. We can now see more clearly, for example, that the idea of legal agency introduced earlier in Section 3.3.1 is the specific kind of agency in the face of political power that is possible only in an order of rule of law, and necessarily absent in an order of rule by law. The reason why is because legal agency so understood is a direct product of the quality of relationship between subjects and officials of the rule of law. It is equally what is necessary to support the subject's acceptance of the authority of law possessed and exercised by the rule of law's officials. These observations will now come with us as we ask why it is persistently the case that some people are missing from – or missing out within – the rule of law.

3.4.1 Available Equally to All?

When the late nineteenth century English constitutional theorist, A. V. Dicey, argued for a strong association between the rule of law and equality, he meant the equality of all before the same law (Section 1.5.1). But when Dicey wrote about the importance of this and other offerings of the rule of law to 'us' (Walters, 2021: 153), who exactly belonged to that 'us'? Women? Children? The peoples of England's then colonies, penal subjects and indigenous persons alike (Lino, 2018)? Or only a very small group of white English men?

It is relatively rare for theorists of the rule of law to pay explicit attention to the people to whom its claimed offerings are denied, in whole or in part.[72] Yet asking who is missing – or missing out – within rule of law thought and practice illuminates much about the tendencies of inclusion and exclusion that animate different ways of thinking about the idea. The reason(s) why certain people have been precariously positioned in relation to the rule of law cannot be answered in the same way for all. Still, the thought developed here is that all non- or partial persons of the rule of law have two things in common. The first is the significance of their status, whether assigned by the social order in which such persons are located,[73] or through the operation of law.[74] The second is the denial of the rule of law's political demand of mutual subordination to law, in their case.

A number of sites of inquiry might have been brought into focus to explore these thoughts, not least feminist (Munro, 2021) and critical race theory (Bridges, 2021) approaches to the rule of law. Here, however, we will bring these observations into relief by reflecting on the place of slavery within rule of law thought.

Slavery

The arguably most well-known appearance of the subject of slavery in contemporary rule of law theory is not really concerned with slavery at all. In Joseph Raz's 'The Rule of Law and its Virtue' (1979: 221), reference to slavery is made within an analysis that builds towards the argument that the rule of law is the instrumental virtue of law: that which makes law more effective, irrespective of the morality or immorality of its ends. It is a powerful example to deploy. Slavery is so self-evidently immoral that the idea that a legal system which denies liberty to particular persons could nonetheless be one committed to the rule of law is sobering. Yet, whether the example ultimately has that effect depends on whether the arguments it is intended to support are accepted (Fox-Decent, 2014: 118–19).

There is much more to be learned for rule of law thought from the example of slavery than its use to support an instrumental philosophical argument might suggest. The first instinct here might be to fix upon the legal character of

---

[72] For a notable exception to this trend, see Shklar's (1987: 1–2) analysis of the inclusiveness of Aristotle's and Montesquieu's rule of law thought respectively.

[73] For example, the status of a slave, a woman, a child, or a member of a particular caste

[74] For example, the status of non-citizen that is central to immigration law, or of the status of the second-class citizen constituted through apartheid laws.

historical 'chattel' slavery, which saw the creation and enforcement of the legal right to hold property in the person of another.[75] For present purposes, however, we might reflect on the relational dimensions of that historical legal institution. Being the object of another's property is not just an extreme manifestation of being acted upon. It constitutes an extreme denial of the possibility of legal agency – agency in the face of political power – that is fundamental to the idea of the rule of law. Revisiting slavery in the context of the present discussion might accordingly invite us to approach the figure of the slave as a person to whom subjectivity within the rule of law has been radically refused.[76] This was Montesquieu's (2001: 263) point when he suggested that by definition the slave 'has no interest in any civil institutions', in the sense of the slave (not) being able to make a claim upon those institutions for their protection. Being the object of another's mastery, Montesquieu reasoned, the slave 'can be retained only by a family law, that is, by the master's authority'.

The advent of legally enforceable property rights in the slave of the kind seen in the history of the United States might be thought to confirm Montesquieu's conclusion that the slave stands outside of the operation of 'civil institutions'. Other aspects of that history, such as the fact that legal restrictions ultimately imposed on slave owners ultimately came to afford slaves certain minimal kinds of legal protection, might complicate this assertion, or at least add nuance to the examination of slavery in a rule of law register.[77] That said, if we return to the analysis of subjectivity to and within the rule of law offered in this part, in which such subjectivity must encompass the legal *and* political dimensions of the idea, the reply would be that whatever minimal legal protections came to be afforded to the slave could be of significance only if they operated to foster legal agency: the capacity to make a law-based demand on political power.

How, then, are we to comprehend the character of a political order that simultaneously sustains forms of full, partial and non-subjectivity, as if along a continuum? Can such an order only make claim to commitment to the rule of law in relation to some people and not others? The difficulties that attend answering this question are the difficulties that attend theorising the rule of law per se (Dyzenhaus, 2022: 297–351). Yet by leading with the question of subjectivity, we are invited to revisit that theoretical endeavour with fresh

---

[75] It is notable that discussions of 'modern slavery' – an institution associated primarily with exploitative labour practices rather than with the property rights in another person associated with 'chattel slavery' – rarely engage arguments about the rule of law. The chosen prism of analysis is instead human rights: Jovanovic (2020). For an exception, see McQuade (2019: 29).

[76] For a recent rearticulation of how slavery has figured within legal philosophy debates that resonates with the reflections offered here, see Neoh (2021).

[77] Fuller offered some preliminary reflections on this point in private correspondence concerned with his claims about the internal morality of law: see Rundle (2012: 112–15).

eyes.[78] In particular, it positions us to engage more fully with the underlying message of Judith Shklar's lament towards what she thought was the relative paucity of political theory concerns within contemporary theoretical treatments of the rule of law (1987: 2–3). Fundamentally, Shklar was worried about the loss of a line of vision towards the political circumstances of subjects in contemporary rule of law thought. But rather than abandon the idea entirely, she demanded a rethink (Shklar, 1987: 16). If the rule of law is not about how a political order can reconcile its power with the personhood of its subjects, then what exactly is it about?

3.4.2 Subjectivity and Legal Form

There is more to understanding the conditions in which the rule of law's core political demand of mutual subordination to law can fail than noticing the consistency with which such failure attaches to people who have been assigned certain social or legal statuses. We need also to pay close attention to connections between subjectivity and form: that is, to how subjects are structurally positioned within the legal and institutional forms through which this failure of mutual subordination occurs.

As we learned in Section 3.2.1, the legal form long presumed to be the hero of rule of law thought – and usually presupposed by it – is enacted rules of general application. The idea that law in a rule of law order is comprised of generally applicable rules is critical to the claim that it fosters the equality of all before the law, as well as to the claim that liberty resides in the spaces where the rules do not apply. By contrast, the legal form long considered the enemy of the rule of law is discretion, ostensibly because it appears to offer an opportunity for the exercise of arbitrary power. Yet as we saw in Section 3.2.2, discretion is more complex than initial responses to it in rule of law theory might suggest, and at least some have insisted that appropriately structured and carefully exercised discretions can be compatible with the rule of law (Davis, 1969: 4, 30).

We return to discretion here to recast this point into one about how not all discretions are the same in relational terms. The kinds of discretionary power within which the rule of law's core political demand of mutual subordination fares the worst tend to be those that see power vested personally in an occupant of political office and exercisable by reference to irretrievably political considerations of the public or national interest. It is not coincidental that these kinds of discretionary powers tend to attach to subjects who occupy a marginalised social or political status, as their ubiquity in immigration law makes clear (Kneebone, 2009).

---

[78] There are many ways through which this revisitation might be pursued, one of which would be to redescribe substantive conceptions of the rule of law (Section 1.3.1) as those concerned to expand the categories of persons to whom its benefits are made available.

From a rule of law perspective, the point to notice about such powers is this. Asymmetries of power will invariably attach to any legal arrangement in which only one side possesses the authority of the state. Such asymmetries can be expected even within a rules-governed political relationship between official and subject, but at least this relationship will be framed by rules known in advance, and any discretion as to the application of those rules will usually be contestable.[79] The form of relation constituted within a discretionary power is entirely different. The crucial feature of choice that is given only to the official displaces the structure of mutual subordination characteristic in an order of rules (Rundle, 2021a: 238). The more inflated the discretion, in terms of favouring the power of the official, the more disenfranchised the position of the subject. Complex discretionary powers like those commonly seen in immigration law operate to radically diminish the subject's agency within the official-subject relationship at the same time as they radically expand that of the official (Wilberg, 2017; Macklin, 2018; Ray, 2021; Rundle, 2021a). Indeed, sometimes the term relationship may barely be applicable – sheer power packaged in 'a tinsel of legal form' (Fuller, 1958: 660) might be a more apt description.

The devices of contemporary immigration law are just one place we might look to develop new frontiers of rule of law thought concerned with granular connections between personhood, power, and form of this kind. The enduring problems of politics and law invent themselves anew in new conditions. Thus, if our thinking about the rule of law is to remain serviceable to emerging challenges, we must always be ready to interrogate our assumptions, reassess our tools, and be open to new ways of seeing if fresh approaches to addressing those challenges are to be fostered.

3.5 Coda: The Provocation from Indigenous Thought

The idea of the rule of law with which this Element has been concerned developed alongside the consolidation of England's colonial empire and the foundational political encounters with indigenous peoples that came with it (Lino, 2018). Those first encounters of largely lawless violence in turn led to the oppressive and discriminatory settler state legal regimes to which indigenous peoples were historically and largely continue to be subjected. Then, as now, those regimes have manifested the very worst excesses of 'rule by law', and more often than not the relationships between officials and subjects they have sustained barely qualify for the description.

We might have turned to the place of indigenous persons within rule of law thought in our discussion of whether the rule of law is equally available to all

---

[79] Recall our discussion at Sections 2.4.1 and 2.4.2 about the rule of law as an argumentative practice.

(Section 3.4.1). The experience of indigenous peoples in England's former colonies deserves its own treatment in relation to that question. As Val Napoleon's work (2022) on the position of indigenous women and girls in the Canadian settler state has illuminated so powerfully, indigenous persons can find themselves excluded from not one but two political and legal orders. They are disenfranchised within the legal and political order of the settler state, and they are *also* disenfranchised within their traditional political and legal orders through the operation of settler law on those traditional orders.

If the idea of the rule of law figures rarely in writings on indigenous political and legal thought, it is not because indigenous traditions contain no idea of law-governed political order (Watson, 1997; Black, 2010; Gover, 2020). What is true, however, is that indigenous conceptions of law-governed political order are organised around patterns of thought that run in very different directions to those we have examined in this Element.

To begin, indigenous political and legal thought does not commence from the figure of the private individual with an interest in their liberty (Borrows, 2016). It commences instead from connections and shared obligations to land. The notion that a person's freedom resides in the spaces where law is not is accordingly nonsensical. So too is the otherness of law that, in the rule of law tradition, is fundamental to its capacity to discipline power. There the law remains outside rather than within us: it is imposed. Indigenous legal and political thought refuses this externality and verticality. Law resides within the land and within the persons who have custodianship of the land. Its relationality needs no emphasis (Graham, 1999; Williams, 2022).

Indigenous persons also do the work of law-governed political order, and its theorisation, very differently to what we have seen in this Element (Friedland & Napoleon, 2015). Drawings, songlines, and stories carry as well as apply the obligations shared by all towards the law and the land within which it resides (Borrows, 2010; Napoleon & Friedland, 2016; Anker, 2017). The written texts so central to rule of law thought and practice have little place.

We conclude, therefore, with a provocation. Both the rule of law and indigenous traditions speak to political orders within which law is assigned a central role. And so, we might ask: how and in what ways might they be able to come together, to find common ground (Davis & Langton, 2016)? Which aspects of our thinking on the rule of law might need to shift to make space for that project? A mutually respectful political and legal coexistence between indigenous peoples and the inheritors of A. V. Dicey's very English ideas depends on more than thoughtful responses to these questions. But if the peoples of those societies are to find a way towards something that, together, they can regard as their law, these are questions that must be answered.

References

Ackerman, B. (2000). The New Separation of Powers. *Harvard Law Review,* 113(3): 633–729.

Allan, T. R. S. (2001). *Constitutional Justice: A Liberal Theory of the Rule of Law.* Oxford: Oxford University Press.

Allan, T. R. S. (2013). *The Sovereignty of Law: Freedom, Constitution and Common Law.* Oxford: Oxford University Press.

Allan, T. R. S. (2014). The Rule of Law as the Rule of Private Law. In L. M. Austin & D. Klimchuk, eds., *Private Law and the Rule of Law.* Oxford: Oxford University Press: 67–91.

Anker, K. (2017). Law as … Forest: Eco-logic, Stories and Spirits in Indigenous Jurisprudence. *Law Text Culture,* 21(1): 191–213.

Aristotle. (2016). Politics: Book III. In J. Barnes, ed., *Aristotle's Politics: Writings from the Complete Works: Politics, Economics, Constitution of Athens.* Princeton: Princeton University Press: 58–92.

Arthurs, H. W. (2005). The Administrative State Goes to Market. *University of Toronto Law Journal,* 55(3): 797–831.

Austin, L. M. & Klimchuk, D., eds. (2014). *Private Law and the Rule of Law.* Oxford: Oxford University Press.

Barber, N. W. (2018). *The Principles of Constitutionalism.* Oxford: Oxford University Press.

Bateman, W. (2020). Algorithmic Decision-Making and Legality: Public Law Dimensions. *Australian Law Journal,* 94(7): 520–30.

Beaulac, S. (2009). The Rule of Law in International Law Today. In G. Palombella & N. Walker, eds., *Relocating the Rule of Law.* Oxford: Hart: 197–223.

Bellamy, R., ed. (2005). *The Rule of Law and the Separation of Powers.* London: Routledge.

Bellamy, R. (2009). *Political Constitutionalism: A Republican Defence of the Constitutionality of Democracy,* 1st ed. Cambridge: Cambridge University Press.

Berger, K. G. (2016). The Supreme Court in Canada's Constitutional Order. *Review of Constitutional Studies* 20(2): 143–164.

Bingham, T. (2010). *The Rule of Law.* London: Penguin.

Black, C. F. (2010). *The Land Is the Source of the Law: A Dialogic Encounter with Indigenous Jurisprudence.* New York: Routledge.

Borrows, J. (2010). *Drawing Out the Law: A Spirit's Guide.* Toronto: University of Toronto Press.

Borrows, J. (2016). *Freedom and Indigenous Constitutionalism*. Toronto: University of Toronto Press.

Bridges, K. M. (2021). Critical Race Theory and the Rule of Law. In J. Meierhenrich & M. Loughlin, eds., *The Cambridge Companion to the Rule of Law*. Cambridge: Cambridge University Press: 357–74.

Carmichael, V. & Webber, G. (2021). The Rule of Law in a Pandemic. *Queen's Law Journal*, 462(2): 317–25.

Carney, T. (2019). Robo-debt Illegality: The Seven Veils of Failed Guarantees of the Rule of Law? *Alternative Law Journal*, 44(1): 4–10.

Cartier, G. (2009). Administrative Discretion and the Spirit of Legality: From Theory to Practice. *Canadian Journal of Law and Society*, 24(3): 313–35.

Chalmers, S. & Pahuja, S. (2021). (Economic) Development and the Rule of Law. In J. Meierhenrich & M. Loughlin, eds., *The Cambridge Companion to the Rule of Law*. Cambridge: Cambridge University Press: 377–405.

Cheesman, N. & Janse, R. (2019). Martin Krygier's Passion for the Rule of Law (and His Virtues). *Hague Journal on the Rule of Law*, 11(2–3): 255–76.

Chesterman, S. (2008). An International Rule of Law? *The American Journal of Comparative Law*, 56(2): 331–61.

Cohn, M. (2021). *A Theory of the Executive Branch: Tension & Legality*, 1st ed. Oxford: Oxford University Press.

Craig, P. (1997). Formal and Substantive Conceptions of the Rule of Law: An Analytical Framework. *Public* Law, (3): 467–87.

Crawford, J. (2003). International Law and the Rule of Law. *Adelaide Law Review*, 24(1): 3–12.

Crawford, L. B. (2017). *The Rule of Law and the Australian Constitution*. Leichhardt: The Federation Press.

Crawford, L. B. (2020). Between a Rock and a Hard Place: Executive Guidance in the Administrative State. In J. Boughey & L. B. Crawford, eds., *Interpreting Executive Power*. Alexandria: The Federation Press: 7–23.

Creyke, R. & McMillan, J. (2008). Soft Law v Hard Law. In L. Pearson, C. Harlow & M. Taggart, eds., *Administrative Law in a Changing State: Essays in Honour of Mark Aronson*, 1st ed. London: Bloomsbury: 377–406.

Davis, K. C. (1969). *Discretionary Justice: A Preliminary Inquiry*. Baton Rouge: Louisiana State Press.

Davis, M. & Langton, M., eds. (2016). *It's Our Country: Indigenous Arguments for Meaningful Constitutional Recognition and Reform*, 1st ed. Melbourne: Melbourne University Publishing.

Dicey, A. V. (1915). Development of Administrative Law in England. *The Law Quarterly Review*, 31(122): 148–53.

Dicey, A. V. (1897). *Introduction to the Study of the Law of the Constitution*, London: Macmillan.

Dixon, R. & Landau, D. (2021). *Abusive Constitutional Borrowing: Legal Globalization and the Subversion of Liberal Democracy*, 1st ed. Oxford: Oxford University Press.

Dworkin, R. (1977). The Model of Rules I. Reprinted in *Taking Rights Seriously*. Cambridge, MA: Harvard University Press. 14–45

Dworkin, R. (1986). *Law's Empire*. Cambridge, MA: Harvard University Press.

Dworkin, R. (2004). Hart's Postscript and the Character of Political Philosophy. *Oxford Journal of Legal Studies*, 24(1): 1–37.

Dylan, L. (2018). The Rule of Law and the Rule of Empire: A. V. Dicey in Imperial Context. *Modern Law Review*, 81(5): 739–64.

Dyzenhaus, D. (2008). Schmitt v. Dicey: Are States of Emergency Inside or Outside the Legal Order? *Cardozo Law Review*, 27(5): 2005–40.

Dyzenhaus, D. (2022). *The Long Arc of Legality: Hobbes, Kelsen, Hart*. Cambridge: Cambridge University Press.

Finnis, J. (1980). *Natural Law and Natural Rights*. Oxford: Clarendon Press.

Fox-Decent, E. (2014). Unseating Unilateralism. In L. M. Austin & D. Klimchuk, eds., *Private Law and the Rule of Law*. Oxford: Oxford University Press: 116–38.

Friedland, H. & Napoleon, V. (2015). Gathering the Threads: Indigenous Legal Methodology. *Lakehead Law Journal*, 1(1): 16–44.

Fuller, L. L. (1958). Positivism and Fidelity to Law: A Reply to Professor Hart. *Harvard Law Review*, 71(4): 630–72.

Fuller, L. L. (1969). *The Morality of Law*, rev. ed. New Haven: Yale University Press.

Galligan, D. J. (1996). *Due Process and Fair Procedures: A Study of Administrative Procedures*. Oxford: Clarendon Press.

Gardner, J. (2012). The Supposed Formality of the Rule of Law. In J. Gardner, ed., *Law as a Leap of Faith: Essays on Law in General*. Oxford: Oxford University Press: 195–220.

Gargarella, R. (2021). Constitutionalism and the Rule of Law. In J. Meierhenrich & M. Loughlin, eds., *The Cambridge Companion to the Rule of Law*. Cambridge: Cambridge University Press: 425–42.

Ginsburg, T. & Moustafa, T. (2008). *Rule by Law: The Politics of Courts in Authoritarian Regimes*. Cambridge: Cambridge University Press.

Ginsburg, T. & Versteeg, M. (2021). Rule of Law Measurement. In J. Meierhenrich & M. Loughlin, eds., *The Cambridge Companion to the Rule of Law*. Cambridge: Cambridge University Press: 494–512.

Gover, K. A. (2020). Legal Pluralism and Indigenous Legal Traditions. In P. S. Berman, ed., *The Oxford Handbook of Global Legal Pluralism*. Oxford: Oxford University Press: 847–75.

Gowder, P. (2018). Transformative Legal Technology and the Rule of Law. *University of Toronto Law Journal*, 68(supplement 1): 82–105.

Graham, M. (1999). Some Thoughts about the Philosophical Underpinnings of Aboriginal Worldviews. *World Views Environment Culture Religion*, 3(2): 105–18.

Grenfell, L. (2013). *Promoting the Rule of Law in Post-Conflict States*. New York: Cambridge University Press.

Hart, H. L. A. (1958). Positivism and the Separation of Law and Morals. *Harvard Law Review*, 71(4): 593–629.

Hart, H. L. A. (1961). *The Concept of Law*. Oxford: Clarendon Press.

Hay, D. (2021). E. P. Thompson and the Rule of Law: Qualifying the Unqualified Good. In J. Meierhenrich & M. Loughlin, eds., *The Cambridge Companion to the Rule of Law*. Cambridge: Cambridge University Press: 202–20.

Hayek, F. A. (2006). *The Constitution of Liberty*, Routledge Classics ed. London: Routledge.

Hayek, F. A. (2007). *The Road to Serfdom*. Chicago: University of Chicago Press.

Hayek, F. A. (2013). *Law, Legislation and Liberty*. London: Routledge.

Hertogh, M. (2016). Your Rule of Law is Not Mine: Rethinking Empirical Approaches to EU Rule of Law Promotion. *Asia Europe Journal*, 14(1): 43–59.

Hickman, T. (2020). The Use and Misuse of Guidance during the UK's Coronavirus Lockdown. https://papers.ssrn.com/sol3/papers.cfm?abstract_id=368 6857.

Hildebrandt, M. (2016). Law as Information in the Era of Data-Driven Agency. *Modern Law Review*, 79(1): 1–30.

Hildebrandt, M. (2018). Law as Computation in the Era of Artificial Legal Intelligence: Speaking Law to the Power of Statistics. *University of Toronto Law Journal*, 68(supplement 1): 12–35.

Hobbes, T. (2017). *Leviathan*, 1st ed. London: Penguin Classics.

Horwitz, M. (1977). The Rule of Law: An Unqualified Human Good. *Yale Law Journal*, 86(3): 561–6.

Howarth, D. (2015). The Politics of Public Law. In M. Elliott & D. Feldman, eds., *The Cambridge Companion to Public Law*. Cambridge: Cambridge University Press: 37–55.

Humphreys, S. (2021). An 'International Rule of Law Movement'? In J. Meierhenrich & M. Loughlin, eds., *The Cambridge Companion to the Rule of Law*. Cambridge: Cambridge University Press: 474–93.

Hutchinson, A. (1999). The Rule of Law Revisited: Democracy and Courts. In D. Dyzenhaus, ed., *Recrafting the Rule of Law: The Limits of Legal Order.* Oxford: Hart: 196–224.

Hutchinson, A. & Monahan, P., eds. (1987). *The Rule of Law: Ideal or Ideology.* Toronto: Carswell.

International Monetary Fund. (1996). *Partnership for Sustainable Global Growth,* Interim Committee Declaration, Washington, D.C. Annexed to Press Release No. 96/49: Communiqué of the Interim Committee of the Board of Governors of the International Monetary Fund. www.imf.org/en/News/Articles/2015/09/14/01/49/pr9649#partner.

Jones, M. L. (2017). The Right to a Human in the Loop: Political Constructions of Computer Automation and Personhood. *Social Studies of Science,* 47(2): 216–39.

Jovanovic, M. (2020). The Essence of Slavery: Exploitation in Human Rights Law. *Human Rights Law Review,* 20(4): 674–703.

Kennedy, R. (2020). The Rule of Law and Algorithmic Governance. In W. Barfield, ed., *The Cambridge Handbook of the Law of Algorithms.* Cambridge: Cambridge University Press: 209–32.

King, J. (2019). Martin Krygier and the Tempering of Power. *Hague Journal on the Rule of Law,* 11(2–3): 363–70.

Kneebone, S. (2009). The Australian Story: Asylum Seekers Outside the Law. In S. Kneebone, ed., *Refugees, Asylum Seekers and the Rule of Law: Comparative Perspectives.* Cambridge: Cambridge University Press: 171–227.

Krygier, M. (2008). The Rule of Law: Legality, Teleology, Sociology. In G. Palombella & N. Walker, eds., *Relocating the Rule of Law.* Oxford: Hart: 44–69.

Krygier, M. (2011). Four Puzzles about the Rule of Law: Why, What, Where? And Who Cares? In J. E. Fleming, ed., *Getting to the Rule of Law: NOMOS L.* New York: New York University Press: 64–104.

Krygier, M. (2016a). The Rule of Law: Pasts, Presents, and Two Possible Futures. *Annual Review of Law and Social Science,* 12(1): 199–229.

Krygier, M. (2016b). Tempering Power. In M. Adams, A. Meuwese & E. H. Ballin, eds., *Constitutionalism and the Rule of Law: Bridging Idealism and Realism.* Cambridge: Cambridge University Press: 34–59.

Krygier, M. (2017). Why Rule of Law Promotion is Too Important to Be Left to Lawyers. In R. Gaita & G. Simpson, eds., *Who's Afraid of International Law.* Melbourne: Monash University Press: 133–68.

Krygier, M. (2019). What's the Point of the Rule of Law? *Buffalo Law Review,* 67(3): 743–91.

Krygier, M. (2021). Democracy and the Rule of Law. In J. Meierhenrich & M. Loughlin, eds., *The Cambridge Companion to the Rule of Law*. Cambridge: Cambridge University Press: 406–24.

Lacey, N. (2021). Populism and the Rule of Law. In J. Meierhenrich & M. Loughlin, eds., *The Cambridge Companion to the Rule of Law*. Cambridge: Cambridge University Press: 458–73.

Lazarus, L. (2018). Doing Violence to the Rule of Law. https://papers.ssrn.com/sol3/papers.cfm?abstract_id=3170649.

Lefkowitz, D. (2020). Global Legal Pluralism and the Rule of Law. In P. S. Berman, ed., *The Oxford Handbook of Global Legal Pluralism*. Oxford: Oxford University Press: 365–83.

Lino, D. (2018). The Rule of Law and the Rule of Empire: A. V. Dicey in Imperial Context. *The Modern Law Review*, 81(5): 739–64.

Locke, J. (1982). XI of the Extent of the Legislative Power. In R. H. Cox, ed., *Second Treatise of Government: An Essay Concerning the True Original, Extent and End of Civil Government*. New York: John Wiley: 81–8.

Loughlin, M. (1992). *Public Law and Political Theory*. Oxford: Clarendon Press.

Loughlin, M. (2018). The Apotheosis of the Rule of Law. *The Political Quarterly*, 89(4): 659–66.

Macklin, A. (2018). Citizenship, Non-Citizenship and the Rule of Law. *University of New Brunswick Law Journal*, 69(2): 19–56.

Marmor, A. (2010). The Ideal of the Rule of Law. In D. Patterson, ed., *A Companion to Philosophy of Law and Legal Theory*, 2nd ed. Oxford: Blackwell: 666–74.

Maxwell, J. & Tomlinson, J. (2022). *Experiments in Automating Immigration Systems*. Bristol: Bristol University Press.

McDonald, L. (2004). The Rule of Law in the New Regulatory State. *Common Law World Review*, 33(3): 197–221.

McMillan, J. (2010). Re-Thinking the Separation of Powers. *Federal Law Review*, 38(3): 423–44.

McQuade, A. (2019). Modern Slavery in Global Context: Ending the Political Economy of Forced Labour and Slavery. In G. Craig, A. Balch, H. Lewis & L. Waite, eds., *The Modern Slavery Agenda: Policy, Politics and Practice*. Bristol: Bristol University Press: 29–46.

Meierhenrich, J. (2021). *Rechtsstaat* versus the Rule of Law. In J. Meierhenrich & M. Loughlin, eds., *The Cambridge Companion to the Rule of Law*. Cambridge: Cambridge University Press: 39–67.

Meierhenrich, J. & Loughlin, M., eds. (2021). *The Cambridge Companion to the Rule of Law*. Cambridge: Cambridge University Press.

Montesquieu, B. d. (2001). *The Spirit of Laws*, translated by T. Nugent. Kitchener: Batoche Books.

Munro, V. E. (2021). Feminist Critiques of the Rule of Law. In J. Meierhenrich & M. Loughlin, eds., *The Cambridge Companion to the Rule of Law*. Cambridge: Cambridge University Press: 340–56.

Murphy, L. (2014). *What Makes Law: An Introduction to the Philosophy of Law*. Cambridge: Cambridge University Press.

Naffine, N. (2003). Who are Law's Persons? From Cheshire Cats to Responsible Subjects. *Modern Law Review*, 66(3): 346–67.

Napoleon, V. (2022). Gitxsan Legal Personhood: Gendered. In G. Pavlich & R. Mailey, eds. vol. 87A of *Interrupting the Legal Person (Studies in Law, Politics, and Society, Vol. 87A)*. Bingley: Emerald. 19–32

Napoleon, V. & Friedland, H. (2016). An Inside Job: Engaging with Indigenous Legal Traditions through Stories. *McGill Law Journal*, 61(4): 725–54.

Nedelsky, J. (2011). *Law's Relations: A Relational Theory of Self, Autonomy, and Law*. New York: Oxford University Press.

Neoh, J. (2021). Law, Freedom and Slavery. *Canadian Journal of Law & Jurisprudence*, 35(1): 223–40.

Ng, Y. F. (2021). Institutional Adaptation and the Administrative State. *Melbourne University Law Review*, 44(3): 889–927.

Ngugi, J. M. (2005). Policing Neo-Liberal Reforms: The Rule of Law as an Enabling and Restrictive Discourse. *University of Pennsylvania Journal of International Economic Law*, 26(3): 513–99.

Nijman, J. E. (2015). Images of Grotius, *or* the International Rule of Law beyond Historiographical Oscillation. *Journal of the History of International Law*, 17(1): 83–137.

Palombella, G. (2010). The Rule of Law as Institutional Ideal. In L. Morlino & G. Palombella, eds., vol. 115 of *Rule of Law and Democracy: Inquiries into Internal and External Issues*. Leiden: Brill: 3–37.

Pasquale, F. (2020). *New Laws of Robotics: Defending Human Expertise in the Age of AI*. Cambridge, MA: Harvard University Press.

Poole, T. (2010). United Kingdom: The Royal Prerogative. *International Journal of Constitutional Law*, 8(1): 146–55.

Postema, G. J. (2011). Implicit Law and Principles of Legality. In G. J. Postema, ed., *Legal Philosophy in the Twentieth Century: The Common Law World*, vol. 11 of *A Treatise of Legal Philosophy and General Jurisprudence*. Dordrecht: Springer: 141–80.

Radin, M. (1989). Reconsidering the Rule of Law. *Boston University Law Review*, 69(4): 781–822.

Rajah, J. (2014). *Authoritarian Rule of Law: Legislation, Discourse and Legitimacy in Singapore*, 1st ed. Cambridge: Cambridge University Press.

Ramirez, S. A. (2013). *Lawless Capitalism: The Subprime Crisis and the Case for an Economic Rule of Law*. New York: New York University Press.

Rawls, J. (1971). *A Theory of Justice*. Cambridge, MA: Belknap Press of Harvard University Press.

Ray, S. B. (2021). Immigration Law's Arbitrariness Problem. *Columbia Law Review*, 121(7): 2049–118.

Raz, J. (1979). The Rule of Law and its Virtue. In *The Authority of Law: Essays on Law and Morality*. Oxford: Clarendon Press: 210–29.

Raz, J. (2019). The Law's Own Virtue. *Oxford Journal of Legal Studies*, 39(1): 1–15.

Rubin, E. (1989). Law and Legislation in the Administrative State. *Columbia Law Review*, 89(3): 369–426.

Rundle, K. (2012). *Forms Liberate: Reclaiming the Jurisprudence of Lon L. Fuller*. Oxford: Hart.

Rundle, K. (2013). Form and Agency in Raz's Legal Positivism. *Law and Philosophy*, 32(6): 767–91.

Rundle, K. (2016). Fuller's Internal Morality of Law. *Philosophy Compass*, 11(9): 499–506.

Rundle, K. (2019). Fuller's Relationships. In Special Edition on 'The Rule of Law and Democracy', *Archiv für Rechts- und Sozialphilosophie (The Journal for Legal and Social Philosophy)*: 17–40.

Rundle, K. (2021a). Administrative Discretion and Governing Relationships: Situating Procedural Fairness. In D. Meyerson, C. Mackenzie & T. MacDermott, eds., *Procedural Justice and Relational Theory: Empirical, Philosophical, and Legal Perspectives*. London: Routledge: 232–51.

Rundle, K. (2021b). The Morality of the Rule of Law: Lon L. Fuller. In J. Meierhenrich & M. Loughlin, eds., *The Cambridge Companion to the Rule of Law*. Cambridge: Cambridge University Press: 186–201.

Sajo, A. (2019). The Rule of Law. In R. Masterman & R. Schütze, eds., *The Cambridge Companion to Comparative Constitutional Law*. Cambridge: Cambridge University Press: 258–90.

Sandro, P. (2022). *The Making of Constitutional Democracy: From Creation to Application of Law*, 1st ed. London: Bloomsbury.

Scheuerman, B. (1994). The Rule of Law and the Welfare State: Towards a New Synthesis. *Politics & Society*, 22(2): 195–213.

Sempill, J. (2017). The Lions and the Greatest Part: The Rule of Law and the Constitution of Employer Power. *Hague Journal on the Rule of Law*, 9(2): 283–314.

Sempill, J. (2018). Law, Dignity and the Elusive Promise of a Third Way. *Oxford Journal of Legal Studies*, 38(2): 217–45.

Seppänen, S. (2016). *Ideological Conflict and the Rule of Law in Contemporary China: Useful Paradoxes*, 1st ed. Cambridge: Cambridge University Press.

Shklar, J. (1987). Political Theory and the Rule of Law. In A. C. Hutchinson & P. Monahan, eds., *The Rule of Law: Ideal or Ideology?* Toronto: Caswell: 1–16.

Simmonds, N. (2010). Reply: The Nature and Virtue of Law. *Jurisprudence*, 1(2): 277–93.

St-Hilaire, M. & Baron, J. (2019). Introductory Essay: The Rule of Law as the Rule of Artificial Reason. *Supreme Court Law Review*, 92(2): 1–45.

Sunstein, C. R. & Vermeule, A. (2018). The Morality of Administrative Law. *Harvard Law Review*, 131(7): 1924–78.

Sypnowich, C. (1999). Utopia and the Rule of Law. In D. Dyzenhaus, ed., *Recrafting the Rule of Law: The Limits of Legal Order*. Oxford: Hart: 178–95.

Taekema, S. (2021). Methodologies of Rule of Law Research: Why Legal Philosophy Needs Empirical and Doctrinal Scholarship. *Law and Philosophy*, 40(1): 33–66.

Tamanaha, B. (2004). *On the Rule of Law: History, Politics, Theory*. Cambridge: Cambridge University Press.

Tamanaha, B. (2008). The Dark Side of the Relationship between the Rule of Law and Liberalism. *NYU Journal of Law & Liberty*, 3(3): 516–47.

Tamanaha, B. (2011). The Rule of Law and Legal Pluralism in Development. *Hague Journal on the Rule of Law*, 3(1): 1–17.

Tasioulas, J. (2020). The Rule of Law. In J. Tasioulas, ed., *The Cambridge Companion to the Philosophy of Law*. Cambridge: Cambridge University Press: 117–34.

Thompson, E. P. (1977). *Whigs and Hunters: The Origin of the Black Act*. Harmondsworth: Penguin.

United Nations General Assembly. (2012). *Declaration of the High-Level Meeting of the General Assembly on the Rule of Law at the National and International Levels*, Resolution, 67/1. New York: United Nations. www.un.org/ruleoflaw/files/A-RES-67-1.pdf.

United Nations Secretary-General. (2004). *The Rule of Law and Transitional Justice in Conflict and Post-Conflict Societies: Report of the Secretary-General*. New York: United Nations. https://digitallibrary.un.org/record/527647?ln=en.

United Nations Secretary-General. (2014). *Strengthening and Coordinating United Nations Rule of Law Activities*. New York: United Nations. www.un.org/en/ga/search/view_doc.asp?symbol=A/68/213/Add.1.

Waldron, J. (2007). Legislation and the Rule of Law. *Legisprudence*, 1(1): 91–124.

Waldron, J. (2008). The Concept and the Rule of Law. *Georgia Law Review*, 43(1): 1–61.

Waldron, J. (2011). The Rule of Law and the Importance of Procedure. In J. E. Fleming, ed., *Getting to the Rule of Law*. New York: New York University Press: 3–31.

Waldron, J. (2012a). How Law Protects Dignity. *Cambridge Law Journal*, 71(1): 200–22.

Waldron, J. (2012b). *The Rule of Law and the Measure of Property*. Cambridge: Cambridge University Press.

Waldron, J. (2012c). Stare Decisis and the Rule of Law: A Layered Approach. *Michigan Law Review*, 111(1): 1–32.

Waldron, J. (2013). Separation of Powers in Thought and Practice. *Boston College Law Review*, 54(2): 433–68.

Waldron, J. (2015). The Rule of Law in Public Law. In M Elliott & D Feldman (eds)., *The Cambridge Companion to Public Law*. Cambridge: Cambridge University Press: 56–72.

Waldron, J. (2016). The Rule of Law. *Stanford Encyclopedia of Philosophy*. https://plato.stanford.edu/entries/rule-of-law/.

Waldron, J. (2021). The Rule of Law as an Essentially Contested Concept. In J. Meierhenrich & M. Loughlin, eds., *The Cambridge Companion to the Rule of Law*. Cambridge: Cambridge University Press: 121–36.

Walters, M. D. (2020). *A. V. Dicey and the Common Law Constitutional Tradition: A Legal Turn of Mind*. Cambridge: Cambridge University Press.

Walters, M. D. (2021). The Spirit of Legality: A. V. Dicey and the Rule of Law. In J. Meierhenrich & M. Loughlin, eds., *The Cambridge Companion to the Rule of Law*. Cambridge: Cambridge University Press: 153–70.

Watson, I. (1997). Indigenous Peoples' Law-Ways: Survival against the Colonial State. *Australian Feminist Law Journal*, 8(1): 39–58.

Webber, G. (2020). The Duty to Govern and the Rule of Law. In C. M. Flood, V. MacDonnell, J. Philpott, S. Theriault & S. Venkatapuram, eds., *Emergency Vulnerable: The Law, Policy and Ethics of COVID-19*. Ottawa: University of Ottawa Press: 175–82.

West, R. (2011). The Limits of Process. In J. E. Fleming, ed., *Getting to the Rule of Law: NOMOS L*. New York: New York University Press: 32–51.

Westerman, P. (2018). *Outsourcing the Law: A Philosophical Perspective on Regulation*. Gloucestershire: Edward Elgar.

Wilberg, H. (2017). Interrogating 'Absolute Discretion': Are NZ's Parliament and Courts Compromising the Rule of Law? *Federal Law Review*, 45(4): 541–68.

Williams, M. S. (2022). Challenging Settler-State Legal Fantasies: Basic Precepts of First Law. In P. Cane & L. Ford, eds., *Cambridge Legal History of Australia*. Cambridge: Cambridge University Press. 61–84.

World Justice Project. (2021). What Is the Rule of Law? https://worldjustice project.org/about-us/overview/what-rule-law.

Zalnieriute, M., Moses, L. & Williams, G. (2019). The Rule of Law and Automation of Government Decision-Making. *Modern Law Review*, 82(3): 425–55.

Acknowledgements

The author acknowledges and pays respect to the elders of the Boonwurrung people of the Kulin Nation on whose unceded land the work for this Element was completed.

Cambridge Elements ⹀

Philosophy of Law

Series Editors

George Pavlakos
University of Glasgow

George Pavlakos is Professor of Law and Philosophy at the School of Law, University of Glasgow. He has held visiting posts at the universities of Kiel and Luzern, the European University Institute, the UCLA Law School, the Cornell Law School, and the Beihang Law School in Beijing. He is the author of *Our Knowledge of the Law* (2007) and more recently has co-edited *Agency, Negligence and Responsibility* (2021) and *Reasons and Intentions in Law and Practical Agency* (2015).

Gerald J. Postema
University of North Carolina at Chapel Hill

Gerald J. Postema is Professor Emeritus of Philosophy at the University of North Carolina at Chapel Hill. Among his publications count *Utility, Publicity, and Law: Bentham's Moral and Legal Philosophy* (2019); *On the Law of Nature, Reason, and the Common Law: Selected Jurisprudential Writings of Sir Matthew Hale* (2017); *Legal Philosophy in the Twentieth Century: The Common Law World* (2011), *Bentham and the Common Law Tradition*, 2nd edition (2019).

Kenneth M. Ehrenberg
University of Surrey

Kenneth M. Ehrenberg is Professor of Jurisprudence and Philosophy at the University of Surrey School of Law and Co-Director of the Surrey Centre for Law and Philosophy. He is the author of *The Functions of Law* (2016) and numerous articles on the nature of law, jurisprudential methodology, the relation of law to morality, practical authority, and the epistemology of evidence law.

Associate Editor

Sally Zhu
University of Sheffield

Sally Zhu is a Lecturer in Property Law at University of Sheffield. Her research is on property and private law aspects of platform and digital economies.

About the Series

This series provides an accessible overview of the philosophy of law, drawing on its varied intellectual traditions in order to showcase the interdisciplinary dimensions of jurisprudential enquiry, review the state of the art in the field, and suggest fresh research agendas for the future. Focussing on issues rather than traditions or authors, each contribution seeks to deepen our understanding of the foundations of the law, ultimately with a view to offering practical insights into some of the major challenges of our age.

Cambridge Elements ⹀

Philosophy of Law

Elements in the Series

Hans Kelsen's Normativism
Carsten Heidemann

The Materiality of the Legal Order
Marco Goldoni

Sociological Approaches to Theories of Law
Brian Z. Tamanaha

Revisiting the Rule of Law
Kristen Rundle

A full series listing is available at: www.cambridge.org/EPHL

Printed in the United States
by Baker & Taylor Publisher Services